The Mourner's Book of Albums

Daniel Scott Tyndal

The Mourner's Book of Albums

poems by

Daniel Scott Tysdal

For Gillian,

Thank you for this opportunity.
I hope you enjoy!

Tightrope Books

Tightrope Books
602 Markham Street
Toronto, Ontario
Canada M6G 2L8
www.tightropebooks.com

Editor: Stewart Cole
Copyeditor: Shirarose Wilensky
Book & Cover Design: Karen Correia Da Silva

Produced with the assistance of the Canada Council for the Arts and
the Ontario Arts Council.

PRINTED IN CANADA.

LIBRARY AND ARCHIVES CANADA CATALOGUING IN
PUBLICATION

Tysdal, Daniel Scott, 1978–
The mourner's book of albums / Daniel Scott Tysdal.

Poems.
ISBN 978-1-926639-20-8

I. Title.
PS8639.Y84M68 2010   C811'.6   C2010-903971-8

In loving memory of my grandpas. Thank you, Grandpa Kay, for encouraging me to type, and thank you Grandpa Spence for believing that what the wrestlers did was real and asking, while we watched *The Spy Who Loved Me*, "How do they get them pictures?"

"We find a place for what we lose."
                    - Sigmund Freud

CONTENTS

ALBUMS FOR THE LOVERS
WHO REMAIN REELING FOREVER

ALBUMS COMPILED FROM WHAT THE BARN
KEPT FROM THE REST OF THE DEBRIS

ALBUMS THAT AWAIT YOUR REPLY

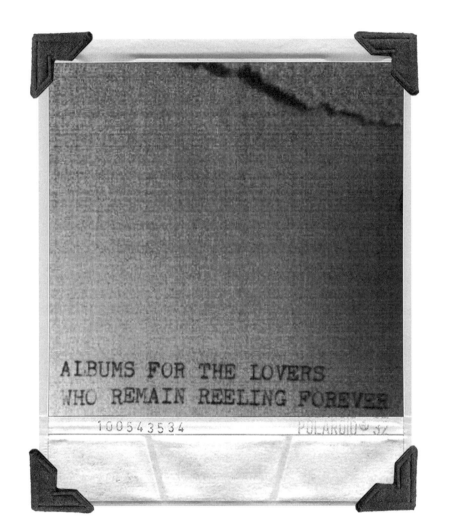

ALBUMS FOR THE LOVERS
WHO REMAIN REELING FOREVER

100543534   POLAROID 37

What is Missing

The night after the boy was kidnapped a group of teens got high and formed the Ministry of Pre-Emptive Memorials. The Minister of Stuffed Animals, The Minister of Flowers, and the Minister of Signed Letters and Anonymous Poems embarked with the others in pairs to locate the goods they'd been assigned to gather. Their work was finished by dawn, and they photographed it, though the memorial lacked the contribution of the Minister of Wreaths (who had been arrested lurking naked in the meat section of an all-night supermarket). The memorial did not bear witness to the boy. What the friends had prepared was meant to brace the world against a calamity yet to come. To keep it ready.

But the next morning a woman who had knit a toque for the kidnapped boy mistook these flowers piled with crucifixes and home made cards as a gathering undertaken for him; she added her offering. She had seen footage from the mall's security camera, on TV first, then online and it doesn't look like a kidnapping. A figure emerges from the crowd of holiday shoppers. They share a few exchanges, man and boy, and then vanish down a hall hand-in-hand. A comment posted online describes the uncoloured blur of their encounter as two ghosts in the afterlife meeting again for the first time. The woman only knew how to knit toques, which was fine, the days were getting shorter. She promised the boy if she learned to knit mitts she would leave a pair to match the hat.

The boy's father had already destroyed the memorial created for the missing child. Neighbours had started it at the entrance of a local park. The boy's father shredded hand-drawn laments and snapped stems as he shouted, He isn't dead! Gathering the debris into a pile, he ignited it using gas from a jerry can and his car's cigarette lighter.

The boy's father also had reservations about the candlelit vigil organized by their church, but he was too busy keeping pressure on the police to imagine the proper protest. His wife spent the whole vigil onstage, though she wasn't really there. Eyes closed on the encouragement each speaker extended to the crowd, eyes closed on the glow of the crowd's flickering support, the boy's mother did what she could to keep close to her son. She sent herself into him. If it had to be this way, it had to; she alone in her love would be the last thing he sensed or saw.

In the passing days, she kept this up, increased her efforts tenfold, even as she and her husband held press conferences, gave interviews to reporters and local talk show hosts. Their boy became a lesson to other children—the don'ts and dos of strangers. Many of these children, this ancient tale new in their ears, wondered what it would be like to be the boy's friend or cousin or sibling or (their stomachs twisting even to think it)—what would it be like to be that, that taken away? A pastor told the story of Christ's empty tomb and said the boy, like that abandoned burial, reminds us of the power of what is missing. One parishioner wondered if this reminder was worth the boy's loss before deciding it was; as the pastor said, the boy teaches us to hope. He will be found. It all will have been for the best.

By then the boy was dead. The death had not been a part of the kidnapper's plan. Before finding the boy the kidnapper had taken pictures of different spaces in his own home. He had secretly pored over the photos at work, trying to decide where in his house the boy would live. To him, great men coined new absences, removed whole peoples, their paces, from the world's endless racing. The room had been right. The boy not. He would never be a great man but that was okay. Soon he would find another boy. Soon he would find another time to take another life and hold it. Soon, in another room, if need be.

Soon the boy was gone from the headlines, gone from small talk, gone from TV. Other events overtook him. The sun's rays grew more dangerous. Rebels barricaded themselves in a classroom of first-graders. A stewardess birthed mid-flight a little one she wasn't even aware she'd conceived. One octogenarian, though, did wake suddenly in the night months later with the urge to pray for the safety of that poor kidnapped boy she had heard about in the news. She pushed through the papers piled in the kitchen, searching for something with his name. But the page was gone, and the boy's name with it. She resigned to saying her prayer not for him alone but for all lost little boys, and maybe for all the lost little girls, which she herself sometimes believed she was, looking in the mirror, because inside, inside living felt the same, but outside, my God, what happened?

Desire, A Lyric Pornographologue of Autoerotic Haunts

Haunt 1: Figures

PHOTO

In the last picture she emailed
she is naked. In return he sent a copy
of the *Kama Sutra*, penciling
on the first blank page, "Here is the map
of that city we can never travel in
because our bodies together compose
its avenues and apartments, its flocks
and bright puddles. As these streets,
I hope, we will meet again
soon." Once he went to the airport
with money for a ticket, prepared
to cross the ocean and surprise her
in her home, and he wonders if
she also dreams of a terminal
without passengers, schedules,
or planes, one holding nothing more
than suitcases, satchels, shoulder-strapped
backpacks crammed tight
in anticipation of all the lands
imagined but never departed for.
It is in this waiting we do not lift off from
where the last we see of love is the photo
of a pose we'll never again enframe
in our own naked poses, the life
we'll never grow quiet with, not in time
for the next uniting flash.

"HOME SWEET HOME"

The emptiness of these houses is filled with concrete. Every room
and nook. Every seat and crevice. The concrete hardens. The roofs
and walls are torn away. The home inside home, stripped of its gaps
for dreams and grieving, is uninhabitable once exposed.

Former owners hand-stitch signs that read, "Home Splayed Naked
Is the Censorship of Home." They purchase houses in other towns
where the face can still waver behind windows watching kin depart
and return and depart again down the front step, where mirrors
still have walls to conceal, doubling the depths for taking life in.

Those who have no choice remain. Their habitats atop the concrete slabs
are subject to the grace of pigeons, rains, neighbours spying
from treetop forts and picture windows. In the hovels tunneled under
the lumps of the old homes, nights are spent debating which rooms
to dig during the day. The concrete in one case collapses an earthen
foundation made porous with the addition of a burrow to a burrow.

The defeated make slabs of themselves. They swallow buckets
of wet cement. The muck solidifies. The skin erodes. It is their hope
to survive as stick people, concrete congregates mawless before the idol
of their concrete hymn. Most end up broken, scattered in chunks
of new stone on the lawn. They are reduced to the fallow for a geology
that measures the harvest of that which starved by asking: "What use
do scavengers find for the ruins?" The hole behind the lips
where chewed food once amassed is tossed solid through a storefront
by looters. Shards are picked clean of teeth and polished for desks
where the papers keep giving themselves to the breeze's tease. Only ghosts

have it worse. At least the lover who lost his love in a now lost room
can weep before the immense surface of the slab. Ghosts have no halls
through which to drag their chains, no more bedrooms of betrayers
or the closets of killers to possess. Abandoned by what they plagued,
ghosts lack even the fractures their phantom voices need to cry, "It was
you."

SONNET

The woman in the sonnet never slept
in the bed in the room her suitors
built for her, the hall of mirrors they polished
to see themselves as seeing her as surf
or hind tethered in a string of their patterns
and longing. After a brief visit to mention
simply, "I was never here other than to say
I wasn't here," what she left behind
for them in blankets was an imprint
of herself, which those who wait for her
curl up inside, and those who hope
to forget her cannot shake clear
of the billowing cloud the linens fake
when snapped against the air.

FABLE

Tell them it's like the fable Aesop told
about the Buffoon who imitates livestock
at the Country Fair, drawing the loudest cheers
for aping the grunts and squeals of a pig,
the fable in which the soil-singed Countryman,
insulted, elbows his way to the head of the crowd
and swears he'll "really show 'em" what pigs
sound like, his squeals so repulsing the crowd
they stone him, dead, drop him to the dirt

without silencing that squeal. And when the Buffoon
rolls the corpse onto its back and yanks
from the Countryman's jacket a wriggling piglet,
those death-flexed fingers still pinching
its ear, tell them the moral of the fable involves
not the squealing Buffoon or the pig's
escape—but the motion of throwing, all apertures
contracting around a stone cast as blindly
as it was chosen. Tell them the grapes plump

and bunched in the painting birds tried to eat
are not edible and never had to be. The curtain
painted on the canvas receives its ovation
not through a miraculous drawing aside,
but by the palms bloodied, the ripped
fingernails with remnants of broken teeth
remaining in those shallow folds
of painted cloth still not torn away.

Haunt 2: Sites

THE BOOK OF DEFORMATIONS

with www.sublimedirectory.com

Here the dead
are handed over
to the dead to give

the living more time
to bury themselves.
Any path undertaken
finds more paths
like in the worst kind
of pirate movie: one map marked with an X
                leads to this same X
                concealing beneath each
                earth another X-marked
map, I mean:

as we scroll through what is offered
our cowering voices are ground
down to elements that barely
fabricate speaking

                          a sound
like trumpets trumpeting trumpets
that strains in a tickertape downpour
over these avenues without any
parades

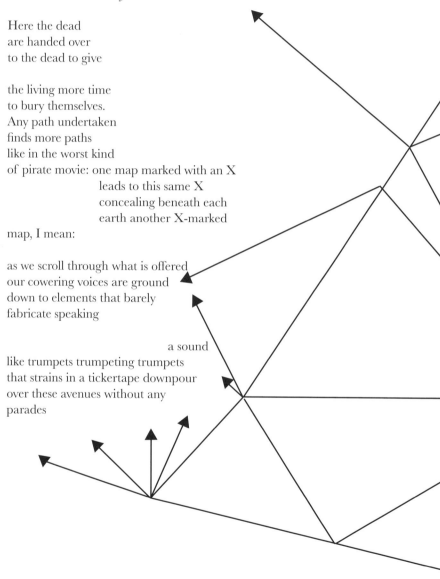

mommy never told me what is my hole for .. 15 pictures of asian beauty gets full of cock and cum 15 movies of two hot babes sharing a hard cock 16 pictures of asian college hottie gets naked in the kitchen Special - 17 movies of Uniform latina sucks big black cock 14 pictures of latin mom lick and drinks cum from her banggers15 pictures of blonde picked up in a bar for hard fucking 12 pictures of tall naugthy teen doing two older men hard 15 movies of hottie jennifer posing topless on the garden 16 pictures of adorable teen in pink panties 16 pictures of big tits gal streching her lips in a huge cock blowjob 20 pictures of sexy blonde teen spreads and fingers her shaved pussy 20 pictures of cute amateur babe gets gangbang on the backseat 16 pictures of cute ebony amateur shows pink parts 15 pictures of bautiful blonde fucked by two big cock guys 15 pictures of miho saito posing nude and erotic 16 pictures of a sweet man massaging oil into his date17 pictures of beautiful petite brunette teen plays with her tight pussy 15 pictures of cute blonde teen in erotic series 18 pictures of busty blonde schoolgirl strips and spreads her pussy 16 pictures of hot teen cutie spreading 16 pictures of petite teen cutie in pigtails teasing Special - 12 pictures of teen takes off her white wet panties15 pictures of flabby asian practice her pussy with some strechings 14 pic- tures of big tit trashy sucking dick till it gives in 5 movies of a guy gets ambused on the road then fucked in the car 20 movies of sex with a hung redneck guy16 pictures of a mariah carey look alike chick pounded hard by punk 14 pictures of stunning blonde fucked her brains out by double black cock 16 pictures of classy ebony babe strips here on sofa 15 pictures of sexy teen amateur plays with dildo 16 pictures of naughty indian teen spreading hairy crack on bed12 pictures of small tit teen girl doing two older men3 movies of young gay riding his male lover 15 pictures of pretty teen blowing dick Special - 19 movies of cock eating bitch gots her full cum 18 movies of porn angel with glasses getting facialized 15 pictures of young couple doing home porn movies 15 pictures of flabby ebony matched into a biggie cocked guy 20 movies of victoria is a wet ebony chick 12 pictures of two guys sucking in the shower room 15 pictures of petite babe takes a shower4 movies of a guy and a chick sucking a cock12 pictures of young britney strips out of tshirt and panties 5 movies of a passenger gets a free ride for sex 16 pictures of fetish gay sucks a cock from his ass 15 pictures of hot petite brunette in panties getting off with her toy 12 pictures of babe gets fucked by guys and guys fucks a gay 16 pictures of bubble butt coed strips for tuition 15 movies of busty ebony babe gets naked 20 pictures of nice plump asian babe 20 movies of horny ebony nurse stripping and showing her pink pussy 15 pictures of sweet ebony babe poses 15 pictures of latina babe in sexy lingerie and black stockings playing with her toy 20 pictures of asian with redheads hair 20 movies of naughty blonde tart gets a big black cock facial20 pictures of gay masturbat- ing on sofa 16 movies of a master punishes his gay slave 20 pictures of hung studs in a tool shop 6 pictures of gay teen soldier does exactly what he is told 20 movies of twink threesome on a bed 16 pictures of my brother shows big erect cock and elastic butts15 pictures of a virgin asian reddens face in her first time 15 pictures of hot mama catching hot fresh cum in her mouth 15 pictures of stunning women fucked and licked by a lucky guy 16 pictures of one typical girl rammed by two raging black cock 16 movies of a professional sex education teacher hardening a cock 16 pictures of a shy guy and a cute chick fucked hard in the end14 pictures of two hot blondes giving pleasure into a guy 16 movies of busty asian housewife fucking with gardener16 pictures of cute blonde teen hot toyed 20 pictures of pretty nice teen spreads her legs for you 16 pictures of perky brunette get naked and shows pussy 12 pictures of guy fucking a babe in front of his wife 15 pictures of busty blonde got rammed by a huge cock 14 pictures of chick in pink sandwiched by two black males 16 movies of two stunning blonde fucked one by one 12 pictures of blonde teen in threesome with two mature men 4 movies of three gay men selecting lots of dildo in the table 15 pictures of shawn and terry sucking cock in the shower 16 pictures of cute blonde twink shows off his sexy nude body 10 movies of brutal gay fucking a guy in the ass with a dildo while sucking15 pictures of asian naughty teen nude 12 pictures of drunk orgy in underground nightclub while in prague 15 movies of teen jogger gets a facial 16 pictures of teen blonde got strike and given a messy cum20 pictures of uk twink

"A GUST OF WIND WHEN LEAST EXPECTED" (GLIMPSES OF THE VOYEUR)

with www.upskirt-voyeur.com

Window: ███ in which ███
███ her hair ███
███ he watches ███
too. Her shoulder ███ porcelain ███ stemming upward
███ through ███
███ yellow ███ coloured ███
███ lace. ███
███ the Girl reaching ███ away ███ arranged
███ A ███ hand in ███ his ███ nonsense.
a ███ is ███ time
███ silk running across ███
looking ███ ? ███ is
world ███ bodies ███
in pieces ███ exposed ███ ?
███ her
███ order
███ positions, ███ a ███ secret
solidarity, ███ at which point ███ his ███
███ tight ███ rotating ███
███ wonder, ███ imagines ███
███ reaching ███ her ███ thus ███
███ in light ███ , ███ dreams ███
███ bodies
███ together ███ remaining ███ apart.
███ see him, ███ static, ███
███ as though ███
rock ███ mantle
but, oh well. ███ his ███ Love
travels ███ that distance ███ no ███
lips ███
███ can ███ own.

22

BEAUTIF: ORPHEUS AFTER EURYDICE
with www.adultfriendfinder.com

Member Profile: Orpheus2006. Am 5'5" with olive skin and hair with a darkness that lasts. Like all true musicians, my voice outlives my songs. (Except the songs I sing for you. They outlast anything inanimate or otherwise.) There's a variety of moth that subsists on the tears of cattle, did you know? Years ago, nobody took the time to inform me, not even during intermission. Knowing this, I more readily would have risked sounding maudlin in asking outright: Where are you?

Looking For: Women; Men; Multiple Patterns; Sirens, don't bother messaging me first, just call. Maenads and vipers need not respond.

Fantasies: *What role-playing scenes do you fantasize about?* Gods-gods; gods-mortals; undead-dead. *What location do you fantasize about?* That dim and quiet whirl in which all things lovely at last go down. *Using the location you chose as the best fantasy setting for a sexual encounter, tell us (in detail) about the encounter. Fact or fantasy?* I imagine Pluto wants another show, Sisyphus hopes to again stand resting with his stone at even my faintest whisper, the dog Cerberus whimpers as at a honey lick, All That Once Was scrambles through this underworld, pushing together a reason for me to sing, a figure of pumice before which everything stands in relief. And when I reach this figure, she follows me to the surface of a soil that opens up on sunlight. Fact: I lose her. Fantasy: I lose her too.

Ideal Person: Someone who doesn't mind if the world is an audience, that any windowsill or petal can praise song's praises. Someone with a wingspan, olden, available. Someone intersected by the historical details often bypassed by myth. Like when Eurydice died her final death, she spoke to me. She said, "It isn't your voice alone that makes you beautif—" but when I turned to watch the lives her lips lived through with each syllable I saw her palms letting go "farewell," ten points of light reflected from fingers tearing from my throat this jumble of dissonant chords.

Sexual Interests: *What factors are most important to you when looking for a sexual partner?* A prolonged look, worn from waiting; fingers that dig at the shoulders as at earth piled into a depth from above; words worth their weight in tunnels. *Besides the obvious, what areas of your body do you consider erogenous zones?* The region that, when touched, draws the cattle into a year-long cry and all the moths slurp up tears until they burst; that whole of a face that turns away no matter how we approach it; the element of a song or its singing that, like a poem, objects; the torsion of an ending that is never quite reached or, if reached, is never quite the end. *Is it true that size matters?* Dimension, no. Distance, yes. *Do you enjoy talking dirty during sex?* What I enjoy is obvious and, yes, it rhymes with bring.

THE BOOK OF YOU
with www.youporn.com

If you haven't got a moneyshot,
you haven't got a porno film.
                    —Industry Adage

Here, if you haven't got a porno film
you haven't got a love life. Here,
you single your own faces out
for the decorums moneyshots incite,
in pairs performing the facial plays
at home and posting the payoffs
online. The cameras have always
lingered in your love, swallowing you
in that slight sense of being watched
that preceded the invention of the lens.
It underpinned the atmosphere caverned
primates found passion in, the hurt
Adam and Eve first claimed, laying down
together as banned and strifed.
But never has this watching been this
material, moulded to grip and shoot down
any pronoun but "you." No need to grasp
at the immutable differences naming holds
fast, the mutable flailing of names. Here,
the flailing insists in each show you spasm
under these linked anatomies, these
megabyte blazons (Canthus ███ ;
Metacarpus ███) that as looker
and lover tear you a new heart.

Haunt 3: Me

I. NOW

—long after the hand divulging the intimacy enclosed
in schoolyard descriptions of the act was drawn
away for the first time, and those metaphors passed
between pals (made mostly of animal injuries, abused
meat) were marvelled over, for their tenor, incommensurate
with what was felt (and long after the anonymous pace
of minutes overtook my sense that I'd escaped

their passing), long after I wiped myself clean, knew
everything had changed, but right around the time
I started searching, immediately, for how
to start again—

II. WEB

In these hours, I am active yet immobile,
a heart that marks life in a way with its rhythm,
but is essentially bound by the web
of cavities and veins in which it's contained.
What contains me are these naked bodies
abridged by their poses like deep lands
made hollow in their migration onto paper
from earth; the pixels my eyes tempt
into unions that bear all the petitions
and fixed responses of a litany but none
of the spirit; the species of beauty
each search-term locates; each linked
click; even that black and white movie's
Dr. Frankenstein I saw on TV years
ago—from oblivion's cavernous fathoms he
retrieved life with hands that stitched
decomposing limbs together, hands
that cupped close to their own
a killer's dead palms.

III. BEYOND

How to fold my eyes around each image
to free up the force that could divide the desired
from such distant and hollow desire. Something
in me surveys this communion, speaks only
of outside or unsightly, of limit or alone, and swears
there's no lasting embrace beyond the captivity
the actors refine in practiced intimacy, their carnal
patter an enclosure you should draw
closer to like an animal made nervous
in the night as its leash winds tighter
with each circle skulked around its stake.

IV. LOOKING UP

I look up from my fist, the noises it makes down there
as dumb and helpless as the things
I can say about them, the repetition endured
to enchant one form; and I see the computer screen
as solid as a world, outshone only by the star
in the end awaiting what could've traveled
but didn't, the passage aroused by the footstep
that never quite seemed able to turn away
from itself. Years ago, a bird must have dropped
a swallowed seed in my fist, because where there are no others
growing, I briefly feel a bloom.

Assemble, Like So (Instructions from the Phrenologist's Lover)

The spirit is a bone.
    —Phrenologist's Adage

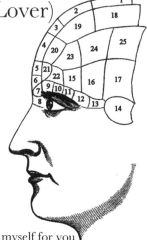

1   Know that not being afraid of exposing myself for you
2   means clearing my skull of obstructions,
3   stopping not with my eyebrows or curls
4   but peeling away the flesh with them,
5   the muscles and tendons, laying raw
6   my bone's subtlest expression of tendency
7   and fate. No lips, true, but no misplaced kisses
8   either. No curls, but no more strands to get tangled
9   in the headboard. Eyelids will be my greatest sacrifice.
10 When I turn from your disappointment—at an ominous
11 dimple in the region of my "Memory of Things,"
12 or an unsightly bump above my "Sense of Metaphysics"—
13 my eyes will slip loose from my skull and wait
14 for my body to emerge searching, this blind bulk
15 palming at air as it lumbers away from
16 what it cannot see to find. Could we ever
17 be otherwise? Just as grips must obey the principles
18 fists set forth for them, so phrenologists' lovers
19 must free their skulls for love. Laughers must fast
20 on sadness. The living must not remain
21 at funerals forever, falling into coffins
22 and ending up buried, while the dead hang around,
23 not even nibbling on the feast laid out
24 at the reception, and leaving the roads un-roamed
25 by anything but flurries.

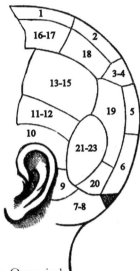

1   Believe that exposing myself will be easy. Our minds
2   are the underneath and ontop of the same
3   shared shard. Both of our sciences are dead,
4   and as seekers we fumble to make them new, to show
5   that what's archaic or killed lingers in more than the gut
6   of what survived to stress over the work
7   of murder and adornment. The hidden, into the hider,
8   trickles. The day phrenologists first put faith
9   in the fact that finger-traced bone said something true
10 about a self, poets pestled words against the world's
11 cranial mortar—its bodies and its things. They made
12 measurable the graced. They said truths are palpable,
13 open to the residue of fingerprints, the endless elasticity
14 of seeing. Imagine there's a day when we are identical,
15 and we travel two centuries in reverse with today's top
16 surgical techniques to smooth all the unfit skulls, to mar
17 the crowns that found themselves on the page labelled,
18 "Just." Imagine the day we are indivisible, studying
19 the snow as though bootprints were traces
20 of a universal synapse, as though snow angels were
21 MRIs of the soul, these icy impressions limning
22 eternity, though the arm-thrashed wings melt
23 and the hemlines in the heat fail to hold.

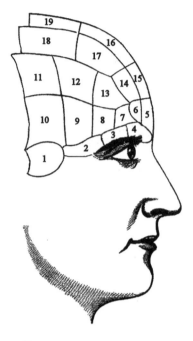

1   Decide whether it matters that I misread you, even ask,
2   "Do you realize I was never moved by the claim
3   that saintly skulls sustained saintly proportions,
4   or that bumps betrayed burglars and hurdlers alike?"
5   If necessary, go further, catalogue what your probes
6   are really after: "the lost origin of inspiration for
7   Darwin's symphony of fitness"; "the phrenological bust
8   that first hinted at a self's sentence to the pulpy perdition
9   of brain matter"; "taught men how to tear a prisoner's skull open
10 and stimulate these neurons to set loose a confession, those
11 to make him howl." You wouldn't have said that last bit,
12 I know. I only wanted my authorship to fit with your authority.
13 I only want to author unfitting actions for your accurate
14 respite: if phrenology had taken a headless subject
15 as its model, would your pioneers have studied
16 the circumference of a neck's mangled stump
17 to determine the contours of a corpse's capacity
18 to do good? Would we range after the faded remains
19 of absences in order to find what is right here?

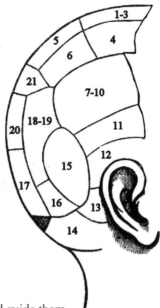

1   Pull my hands to your skull and guide them,
2   teach them a way to get free from touching
3   themselves, their strangling of the sources
4   of any living adhesions, like the self-study
5   the scream unleashed on itself—ears sheltered
6   by scalp-scouring hands as the voice ripples
7   the world away in waves of many-volumed
8   scars (as though making a friend of horror
9   meant only making ourselves horrific (as though
10   hope were truly effaced by the gilding despair
11   that keeps it hidden)). Make us fit
12   together. Make us as malleable as the dolls
13   redeemed in the dream of the child who
14   lost them. Fingers must fight through the canopies
15   of skeleton and penchants that keep them
16   from grasping the hand that ascends
17   from elsewhere. Each sigh is the silhouette
18   of such tactility. Each kiss lights a small cinema
19   on our skin, a home for the movie
20   with the lovers who remain reeling forever
21   in their failure to ever fall apart.

For the day I die, I leave you these instructions.
In the age when no nearness remains squinting
around our wishes, and the only tangling left
are the hairs still tangled in the headboard, strip
my skull clean for real. Then cut from these pages
the words I have written and paste them in the places
marked out for them. Or ink each phrase
over my cranium by hand so the skull can express
unequivocally the bond the longings no
longer lingering inside wanted to be true. Break
these lines into pieces and assemble, like
so, , the way you asked me to assemble
in you assembling in me, whether after waking
together late in the morning or while passing
our hands through the clear of our bodies
in the night we drank and clutched and cursed
and collided and flickered and fell to sleep.

Interlude

TWO FACE, THE TWO-FACED KITTEN

His name is Two Face, the two-faced kitten!
—CNN Reporter

The prow of a great ship, the sharp edge
of an iceberg slicing through the ocean's cool split
between sky and deep, share the same angle
as this calicoed slant that links the cat's
squinting visages. "He's not the bad guy
in this tale," the crack reporter glows, signing off
on the miracle birth, "He's the hero!" The tongues
in the last shot lap milk. Both faces feed.

The world's not always this kind to its mongrels.
Food eludes the organs born outside the skin
when the foetus is kneaded by the radiant touch
of uranium. The daddy's mistake with his daughter
gets no dinner, or a bed to be sent to without it,
only an earthy hovel dug miles from the plots
of buried kin. Others are too close to their kind,
too purely this and not purely that, and the mass graves
they share in ditch and jungle and field are slight
and electric, the milky swirl of the universe snapped
from the seat scientists dream at the cusp

of all things. It was the Romans who built this,
a doorway with faces paired up top to spy
on storms past and future, even though the present,
unwatchable, gores us with torrents as we crouch
in its threshold. Whine, and the chorus is apt to cry:
"Let those who know the doors we cannot build
craft the next jamb." Once, on acid, my friend
knocked himself up after finding a vagina moist
between his ribs, and he told me the child
would have his eyes, and that all us two-faced
bastards could now finally live as one
for millions and bazillions of years.

Each Shall Pay[1]:

TRANSCRIPTION OF THE FRAGMENT OF AN ANONYMOUS
MANIFESTO FOR THE HOMELESS, DISCOVERED IN TORONTO,
ONTARIO, ON AUGUST 31ST, 2007, CORNER OF QUEEN AND
STRACHAN AVE. AT ABOUT 8P.M., THE CONDITION OF THE
SCRAPS BAD, WELL, THE PAPER PUDDLE-STAINED, BUT AT THE
VERY LEAST TWO PAGES REMAIN FOR TRANSMISSION

Dedication

These words are dedicated to sparing
change. They don't beg for coins, but ask for
the excess of change itself—they demand
you ask that change is spared
from its sacrifice to the status
quo. For those haunted by visions
of razor-sharp street cleaners,
these words are tools to undo
your pursuers. With these words,
old tramped-out shoes and newspaper
rinds will no longer contain
your complaints. With these words
you will cast out your oppressors
from where they lie stuffed
and secure inside Jonah's belly inside
the belly of the whale. To you
who have never paid or received, to you
who are the burnt offerings
of paying and receiving, these words
are given, dedicated to the name
of your payback. Let these words
coin you. As they carry you carry
them, in that plastic bag, the one
you lowered over your head in the rain.

---

1 On what one can only assume is the title page of the three page document, the Hebrew word ונתנן is printed. The word, according to the rabbi I shared the fragments with, translates as "each shall pay." The palindromic composition of the word is critical, he pointed out, because it reminds us that charity moves in two directions. One receives as one gives. One who gives now may later need to receive. A poet friend I shared this transcription with said the word should not read "pay" but "give."

VII. Final Note

If there are to be poets, let them be you. Write the real mystery of suffering, a poem that holds the terminal terminal, afflicted with rising and returning, dying from it—this history that subsists in what is remembered like the unborn twin (all partial fingers and mealy bones) the living twin's fetus grew around and consumed. Make this consumed thing born. If change is made from dollar bills, let your complaints and howls and dreams and repeals serve as the first universal currency *(Figure 11, 12)*. The palms you force your worth into—whether they want it or not—must learn true prophets never choose to be chosen. What you purchase, what you make of the world's exchanges, erases you. Nothing afterward will have clues for intuiting there was once such a thing as this scream:

Figure 11 – Front (obverse) of bill.

Figure 12 – Back (reverse) of bill

Dahlia's Dead

ON THE GENESIS OF "DAHLIA'S DEAD"

Dahlia and me were high school sweethearts. Not the "I love you now and forever" kind. We were off-and-on-and-off-and-on- agains. After graduation, we thought we'd split for good until I found myself broke and jobless and she got me a gig slinging drinks with her a few nights a week at Bugsy's Bar and Grill. This was back in Moose Jaw in the summer of '96. Bugsy's was about the length of the number of cigarettes you could smoke in an hour lined up end-to-end.

We'd met in grade nine, assigned in Art class to paint the same football player in the athlete-crammed mural outside the gym. Working together after school, we coloured him the crimson and gold of our uptown enemies, Central Collegiate. "A disgrace," the Vice- Principal said when he threatened to suspend us. Dahlia didn't talk to me for a month after I repainted our player the green and orange of Peacock Tech. That was how it went for the next four years. The things we made drove us apart and forced us back together. There was the stage adaptation of Taxi Driver (shut down after opening night), and the t-shirts we designed based on de Sade's murderous passions (banned within minutes from our high school's halls).

Working at Bugsy's was no different. Comics became our thing. I wrote. Dahlia drew. We started one about the time we dropped acid with our friends and got lost in the Science Centre, another about Dahlia's struggles growing up a first-generation Canadian, another that looked at the quirks and explosions of the angels and weirdoes we served tending bar. We didn't finish any of them. Dahlia went to the University of Saskatchewan to study art in the fall. I went nowhere. Night after night I blended three-dollar daiquiris and emptied the ash from the trays that surrounded the VLTs into an old, label-less coffee tin.

I only saw Dahlia one more time before the accident. She invited me to spend my day off with her in Saskatoon after we missed one another at Christmas. She loved university/wished I'd come with her/was really getting into photography. There were so many new possibilities we barely wasted a second with sleep. For the next two weeks, we spoke on the phone every day. We planned this. Revised that. Decided she should come home to stay with me during the February break. She never made it back. On the last Saturday of that January, a drunk driver killed her and her friend. Separate cars departed from separate nights of revelry. They collided in the same snowstorm on the same ice-wreaked street.

The murderer and his friend, though seriously injured, both survived. The driver, it turned out, was a pro. The night he killed Dahlia and her friend he was driving without a license, having lost it after receiving three previous DUIs. I could just see him, three sheets to the wind, crawling into the car as he slurred, "Who needs a fucking piece of paper?" I avoided hearing any details about Dahlia's death. I couldn't bear it. Even the closed casket told me more than I wanted to know. That evening, outside for a smoke at a gathering of old classmates, I overheard someone say Dahlia had shot clear through the windshield. The guy said it like he was sharing some marvellous scientific fact about magnets or meteorites. The next time he came into Bugsy's I broke a glass against his face. I lost my job and was threatened with criminal charges when the manager looked back through the security tapes. I'd been serving drinks to myself as much as the customers ever since Dahlia's mom called, crying, "My baby's gone."

I moved to Calgary—of all places—to get clean. I had a born-again cousin who worked the rigs for long stretches. He rented me a room in his new condo for cheap. I fed the fish. Promised to say my prayers. I made the transition from bartender to barista and attended AA meetings three nights a week to fill the empty hours.

It was almost two years after my last drink that I met Marin. She'd only been attending the Tuesday meetings at Christ's Church for a few weeks the night I stood and said, "Today's been the hardest yet." The guy who killed Dahlia had gotten off. Second-degree murder was the verdict. A few years. Not life. Marin asked me right after if I wanted to grab a bite to eat. The late dinner at Smitty's turned into a late coffee, later refills, breakfast. After that, she answered her phone every time I called to say I needed to be stopped. That went on for weeks—that need. With her help, I beat it.

I liked spending time with Marin. She listened. She slept on the couch without complaint the nights my cousin was home from the rigs. She didn't know boo about Dahlia but she let me babble on about her, even asking questions, looking closely when, for the umpteenth time, I showed her my small collection of Dahlia's artwork. Mostly, though, I liked Marin because she was nothing like Dahlia. She was older. She was unapologetically inward. She preferred a long run to a gallery stroll. Where Dahlia's olive skin was spotted with acne blooms, Marin's fair face was unblemished, perfectly smooth. She looked like what I needed. Someone completely different. Something new.

The television exposed her. It was my cousin who caught it. He was watching a local Real Life Miracles program. In this segment, medical experts and family members could not explain how a child in

Saskatoon, who had twice been declared dead on the operating table, survived an attack by wild animals. During one of the interviews with the actual surgeon (as opposed to the actor who played him in the re- enactment), my cousin saw in a bed in the background a woman who looked just like Marin. Marin with a thick gash running from her forehead to her jaw. The same program ran again on the same station in a different time zone so my cousin DVRed it. I watched that samesliver of the recording over and over. I knew without a doubt that it was her.

When phone calls to the U of S College of Medicine got me nowhere, I drove straight to Saskatoon. The receptionists at the hospital were no more helpful in person and an administrator I tracked down threatened to call the police. A guy in supplies, who'd happened to hear about my request, said he'd been in AA with Marin following her release from the hospital. He told me the truth. Marin had been drunk in the front seat of the car that killed Dahlia. She'd gotten pretty messed- up herself in the crash, splitting her face open and breaking her leg. But doctors had worked the most cutting-edge magic. The scar on her face. Gone. The scar on her leg. Gone. Not a trace.

I started back to Calgary, the gas pedal pinned, ready to demand Marin pay. But for what? For riding in that car? For witnessing Dahlia die? For being responsible for . . . what? Confused, I called her from a payphone at a gas station in Lloyd. We hadn't spoken in days and I could tell by the way she answered that she knew that I knew.

"Did you see her?" I asked.

There was a long pause.

"Yes," she said.

"What do you want from me?"

There was another long pause.

She hung up.

I drove straight to her apartment when I got back to the city. For three days, I waited in the hall, sleeping in my car, quizzing her neighbours. She never came back.

It only took the one drink. When I wasn't mixing and sipping, I wrote. When I wasn't chugging, I wrote. Blinking my way out of a blackout, I wrote and wrote and wrote. In notebooks. On napkins. Maybe even on bathroom stalls. What I had with me when my cousin sent me back home to Moose Jaw remained in my suitcase until I rediscovered it in the spring of 2003, just before taking off to South Korea. I dumped the scraps in my box of old drafts and abandoned projects. They were too raw to bother reworking. Too raw to publish as they were. Or so I thought until today.

Today, at the Clint Roenisch Gallery on Queen West, just

north of where I live now, I changed my mind. Or better: my mind was changed for me and I decided to include the 5 pieces that follow. I give them to you as I left them. It was a photo by a guy named Burman that did it. His whole thing is the dead, the dead as they've been kept by different cultures from different times: the musculature of a skinned torso, jarred testicles, a cradle-ridden, mummified child. In his glossy, shining images, he blows his subjects up to the size of two big engines tied together side-by-side. The photo that really got me shows a skeleton, in profile, crouching bird-like, bony arms tucked against its bony thighs. Mirrored in the reflective black of the background, I saw the photo on the wall opposite, the head of a man on a pedestal, and with it—startling me—my own floating, ghostly face.

Daniel Scott Tysdal
Toronto, ON
(July, 2010)

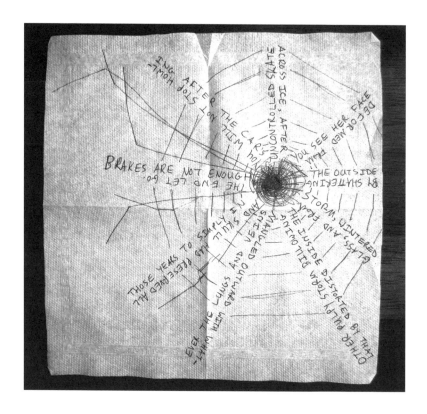

Text: Brakes are not enough. You will not stop howling after the car's uncontrolled skate across ice, after you see her face deformed from the outside by shattering storm, wintered glass, and from the inside distorted by that other, pulpy storm billowing mangled outward with whatever the lungs and veins and skull had preserved all those years to simply in the end let go.

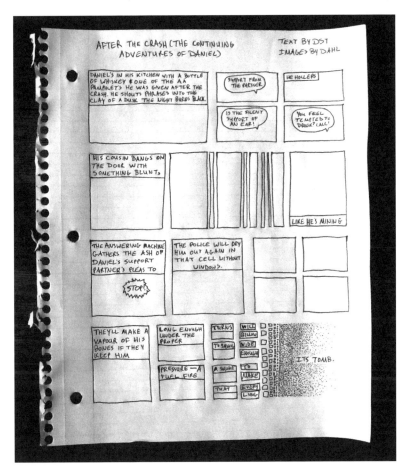

Text: Daniel's in his kitchen with a bottle of whiskey and one of the Alcoholics Anonymous pamphlets he was given after the crash. He shouts phrases into the clay of a dusk the night burns black. "Support from the partner," he hollers, "is the silent support of an ear!" "You feel tempted to drink? Call!" His cousin bangs on the door with something blunt like he's mining. The answering machine gathers the ash of Daniel's support partner's pleas to stop. The police will dry him out again in that cell without windows. They'll make a vapour of his bones if they keep him long enough under the right pressure—a fuel fire turns to smoke, a smoke that'll billow wide enough to make every lung its tomb.

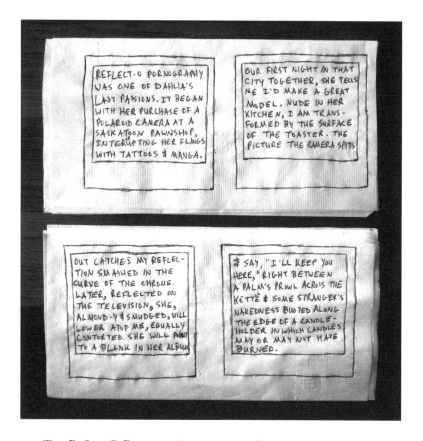

Text: Reflect-O Pornography was one of Dahlia's last passions. It began with her purchase of a Polaroid camera at a Saskatoon pawnshop, interrupting her flings with tattoos and manga. Our first night in that city together, she tells me I'd make a great model. Nude in her kitchen, I am transformed by the surface of the toaster. The picture the camera spits out catches my reflection smashed in the curve of the chrome. Later, reflected on the television, she, almond-y and smudged, will lower atop me, equally contorted. She will point to a blank in her album and say, "I'll keep you here," right between a palm's prowl across the kettle and some stranger's nakedness buoyed along the edge of a candleholder in which candles may or may not have burned.

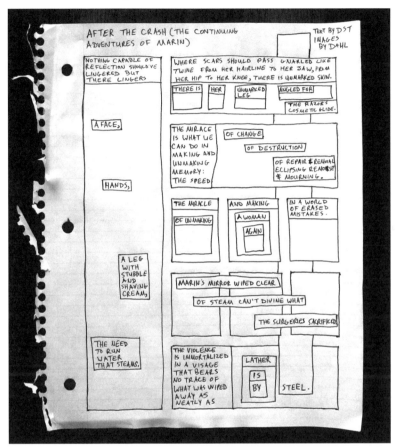

Text: Nothing capable of reflection should have lingered, but there lingers a face, hands, a leg with stubble and shaving cream, the need to run water that steams. Where scars should pass gnarled like twine from her hairline to her jaw, from hip to knee, there is unmarked skin. There is her unmarked leg angled in the tub for the razor's cosmetic glide. The miracle is what we can do in making and unmaking memory: the speed of change, of destruction, of repair and removal eclipsing remorse and mourning. The miracle of unmaking and making a woman again in a world of erased mistakes. Marin's mirror can't divine what the surgeries sacrificed. Marin's mirror wiped clear of steam cannot divine what several surgeries worked to erase. The violence is immortalized in a visage that bears no trace of what was wiped away as neatly as lather is by steel.

Text: We agree on that one thing. Drink is a hammer. It pries at each nail these days drive into your chest. It's like taking a hammer and pounding those nails straight through your soul into nowhere.

ADDENDUM

A week before this book went to press, I spoke
to Dahlia's mom. I told her about the poems.
She asked me to include a story I'd never heard.
As a child, Dahlia nurtured obituaries in place
of pets. She fabricated death notices for birds
and beasts she never in the first place possessed
to lose. She invented a sophisticated cockatiel
who chirped her name when it was time
to rise for school, a border collie who saved her
from slipping through cracked sheets
of frozen water. As a favour to circling vultures,
and to expose the promiscuity of skins in their decay,
she pretended her imaginary dead pets
remained carcasses unburied at the edge
of the garden rather than buried bones,
the breadth of the backyard's burgeoning life
pierced with a stillness so singular it defied
what the siding and shingles asserted to be
the nascent relation of divided hides.
If lightning were to have struck her fantastical pile
of remains, she had known that none of the paws
and fins and wings decomposing into this dreary
chimera would have twitched awake, but in one obit
a newt taken too soon to the pile startled the sky
when parrying thunder slithered from its slender throat.

The Open Toll

FAIRYTALE
written on the occasion of the birth of William Hudson Frank

Robots bolt shut robot chests on robot
hearts, bind robot pieces to robot parts,
their generation of generations
repeated without error, tear, or chance
of loss, the nature of maker in made
retained in flawless features and clockwork
firing frequencies of immortal robot sparks.

The fairies bear the shotgun-birth of squid
and seahorse in the air. Absence-wounding,
their bursts of babies cloud the trees with rains
of wings more varied but as multiplous
as leaves, while ogres birth their little ones
mature like foals, the ogrelings warted
and fanged and falling and wobbling up
with roars to suckle at the broken throats
of fauns, and growling graze the forest edge
for village children who stray too far from home.

Ghosts are brought to life by death, and zombies
dead brought back to life by mauling zombie
chomps. While gods are men remade by mountains,
oceans, crows, and fire, and constellations
borne by gods eye-cast onto the shining
stars. The stars are stones from nothing polished
and tossed into the nothinged pocket
of that God the fear of nothing pleaded, "Live."

How puzzled are stars and gods and zombies
faced with the peculiar human crawling
into life? How fairytale-fitting must
this chance and uncontrolled invention hum
for robot kids, their robot chums, snuggled
in tin blankets with their circuits whirring
for all the swimmers setting out to win
a single prize? One child of a million-
babied fairy carved this lone fantastic

finger of a human mom grasped wrinkly
by the life she birthed, while minutes old, one
ogre filled with glee believing he could
be this palm-sized wart-free babe, too cradle-
bound to pounce from out of dew-dropped branches
and tackle shadow-grappled paths, that new-
eyed squinting strung to the unpoppable
balloon of the sun.

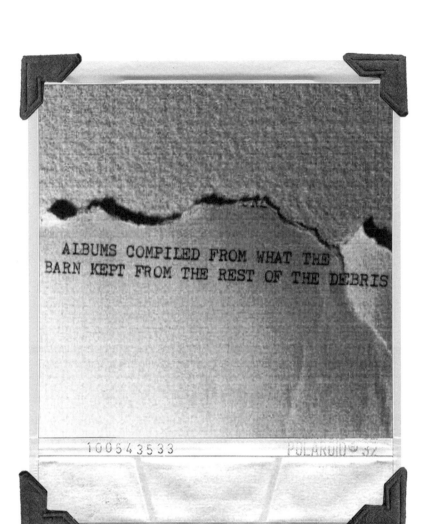

ALBUMS COMPILED FROM WHAT THE
BARN KEPT FROM THE REST OF THE DEBRIS

100543533   POLAROID 32

Videos for Children

There are more cameras than signs
of protest at the G20 rally on 27 June at 1:10 pm
in Queen's Park. Rain falls on the 5000+ assembled
peacefully. It's 2 hours before the calm will fizzle
and the press's pre-protest supplications will in turn
be worshiped with burnt offerings from the Black Bloc:
4 scorched police cars, glass smashed (from the flash
of the Zanzibar strip club's marquee to the siren-logoed
panes of "Charbucks"). The bodies of American
Apparel mannequins will lie dismembered in the streets
as the store is freshened up with faeces. For now,
we march south, then make a right on Queen,
while the black-clad kids who will set the core ablaze
move among us, manic as the dust a bike kicks up
playing rocket ship on dirt roads. They plot their non-plot
in kerchiefs and masks and scan for a way to break
the bored, mortar gaze of the wall of cops who watch us
pass. (You will find pics on Flickr of what I see: the Bloc;
the cops; the woman who, like a bouquet-tossing bride,
releases bunches of balloons as if to show us
which skyscraper is the next to wed; the pink,
snapping manes of the C.U.P.E. flag brigades;
the oversized coat hanger borne for blocks
by ten hands, the burden of maternal health (the hook
of the thing bobs in the air, a fierce
antennae transmitting the torment of life scraped

free.)) Grandmothers Against War can't stand the drone
of Local 183's vuvuzelas. Drummers from groups
with diverse agendas join in one rhythm with horns,
whistles, shouters, singers, the rattle of a Nestea can
a young woman fills with change and shakes. One granny
repeats the rhyme, "Hey Hey / Ho Ho / Stephen Harper's
got to go," while an amp cranked full blast scraps
a Palestinian woman's voice with distortion. The kids in all black
taunt their foes with the cry, "Police State," pissed off at how
remote the cops look, like the fuzz are dreaming of kicking
their feet up with a nice pint while the Yanks take on
Ghana in the World Cup (a game the Black Stars will win

2-1 in extra time). I talk to a guy handing out flyers no one
wants and he says tomorrow he's protesting people who take
pictures at protests. "Tourists," he accuses. Not even shots
of Mohawks at Oka or the Tank Man of Tiananmen Square
can sway him. "It's not the same," he spits then takes off,
kicking at the rain-soaked flyers his fellow activists
grabbed and let go without learning "THE TRUTH
THE OIL COMPANIES DON'T WANT YOU
TO KNOW." With the mad, moping slump
of his shoulders, he could be the Great Creator sifting
through the souls we surrendered to snapshots
to secure a more material eternal life. The iPhones
and Canons of curious consumers, of scribes
professional and amateur, outnumber the cops 2-to-1
on Queen. (This reminds me of what my friend said once
about Bing: "the most listened to voice in the long life
of the world." This hour is my face's most captured.)

By 2:00 p.m., the cops are antsy. Peaceniks threaten
to ruin the show, stalling the staging of the most
ancient drama: the masked against the masked. They've
stuck to the script, not only reducing to a ghost town
our life-dappled streets in the days that led up to
the standoff, but improvising their cage-filled jail
in the Toronto Film Studios. (Where better than a place
of make-believe and special effects to stuff "trash"
into trash-strewn bins, to surveille the private parts
of people the law says expose, the law says,
"You'll just have to piss in front of us when you can't
hold it"?) By ten after, the march is a po-mo production
of *Hamlet*; Fortinbras rushes onstage from
the wings to shout, "Go, bid the soldiers shoot,"
before Bernardo's had a chance to open the play
and ask, "Who's there?" The cops shove, bark, slow
the march to a crawl. Without cause, an officer grabs
my friend's sister's purse and mutely tosses it
into the ocean of black behind him. He dares her to fish
and get caught. This is basic Chekhov: "You can't
put a truncheon in the street in the first act, etc." (Later,
the spotlights of their fists will make her friend a star.)

It's heading north on Spadina, the police still escorting us
at a packed-sardine-pace to keep our mass well-shelled,
when I bump into Kat. She says something about this
being what 1.2 billion bucks buys you: the priciest work
of art of all time. Forget Hirst's 50 million pound
diamond-studded skull, forget "Massacre of the Innocents"
or Pollock's "No. 5." Harper is the new Christo is Kat's
theory. "The people want to reclaim the seat of power,"
she says, "so Harper lets them live it. Walk in a big expensive
circle, change nothing. Repeat." Like the finest details
of the Reichstag vanishing behind a shining, fabric crust,
the particular motives of the marchers are gone—
this barista's quarrel with cash is banished with
this Ethiopian dad's shock at the dictator
who disappeared his son being welcomed to the G20
as a world leader. Kat's boyfriend asks if this
makes neo-Modernists of the Black Bloc. (Sounds right—
I bet they took their name from a lost Malevich
after deciding to impose this return of political action
to its roots, *sans* cause (i.e., origin) or cause (i.e., ideal),
imposing the rule of the purity of the form of one shape
coming down with blind, absolute force against another

shape.) Fire is a simple thing. It's democratic and free,
as skilled at scorching assets as it is at torching
cop cars. We're heading east on College when news comes
that it's started south of us on John. The officers are donning
their gas masks as the Black Bloc begins its game
of Red Rover in pursuit of the miles of security fence
that call them over. What would one of these Bloc-ers say
if he made it? If he got not just within spitting distance
of the fence, but through it, past the fortressed walls
of the Metro Toronto Convention Centre and into the room
where world leaders breathe feeble and unreal
in the flesh. What if instead of banks to paint with
slogans ripped from Tinsel Town pictures, instead of
photo-journalists to smack for snapping the mayhem, this one
dissenter was given the floor? What if each leader and lens
in that meeting waited eagerly to embrace his every word?
What would he say? How about you? (Me? I'd describe
the one thing I'd shoot right now if I owned
a camera. Just up ahead, there's this woman with a sign raised

high in the air. It's the tattered flap from a cardboard box.
She made the sign so quickly she didn't scratch out
what she'd scrawled back when the box was packed
with her things. All of us who trail her read "Undies &
Videos for Children." I can't see what's on the other side.)

Last Flight of Sergeant Deadhead, The Astronut! (A Message in a Bottle)

ON THE GENESIS OF "LAST FLIGHT OF SERGEANT DEADHEAD, THE ASTRONUT! (A MESSAGE IN A BOTTLE)"

I found my uncle's writings in the loft of the barn. My father had recently sold the original homestead, the land his great-grandfather had settled in 1907. We were trying to decide what to take with us and what to haul off to the nuisance ground. Bails had long ago given way in the loft to back issues of Life magazine piled among rotted hockey cards, the guts of outdated machinery dusted with the husks of pigeons and misgiven gifts too gaudy to keep inside (like the geisha-covered blinds an aunt had brought back from what she still referred to as the "orient"). The initials on the crate of writings read, "SDH." My father said right away this was Edmund's.

Before that afternoon, my father, or anyone else for that matter, hadn't said much about my great uncle. I knew he'd served in the Second World War, that he'd never married. My dad was a boy when Edmund died so most of what he knew came from eavesdropping or the gossip his mother shared when she was sure grandpa wasn't listening.

Edmund had come back from the war with a secret. My grandfather, kept out of the service by a blind eye, had only needed a bottle of Swenson hooch to get it out of him. Edmund said they'd been at the front when it happened, he and another private buried body-deep in a foxhole. Ol' Sammy, Edmund called the kid when he was boozing, and Sammy Diver Hades when he sobered up.

They were sleeping through lookout when Edmund woke to the sound of an advance from the east—Germans coming straight at them. He called into camp and the order came to fall back. But it was too late. The Germans were within spitting distance and would pick them off for sure if they retreated outright. He woke Sammy, gave him the bad news, and then lied. He and Sammy were to split up, he said, inventing orders, one heading north into the woods, the other south. They needed to catch the Krauts in a crossfire. Sammy disappeared in the trees. When he drew fire, Edmund escaped.

Edmund went in seclusion for close to a decade after making this confession. It was after my great-grandfather passed away, just before my dad's birth in 1954, that my grandfather had had enough. Edmund wasn't much more than a whiskey-pickled hermit by then, working odd jobs here and there but spending most of his time getting drunk and scribbling little songs and poems. My grandfather couldn't afford a hired man. He decided to get in touch with Sammy's family that winter to ask them to grant the reprieve their dead son never could.

That's how my grandfather learned the real secret. In the young man's hometown, there had been no Sammys in recent memory, no Hadeses either. The name didn't ring a bell with the men Edmund had fought beside. The army replied after my grandfather's second letter. No one with the surname Hades had served in the Canadian armed forces, let alone been reported dead.

Edmund called my grandfather a liar. The army was filled with liars. Sammy had been a flesh and blood soldier. Edmund could prove the military was hiding something. He was banned from the Legion after attacking a fellow veteran who said their brigade never even advanced that far into France. At a Remembrance Day service in 1960 a pigeon was set free, my dad couldn't remember why they hadn't used a dove. Edmund shot it back down to earth.

It was while serving his short stint in jail for this incident that Edmund started writing down his theories: Sammy was an emissary of the righteous sacrificed by his leaders; he'd memorized the blueprints needed to avert the Cold War and had to be rubbed out. Everything became a sign of Sammy. Edmund saw the ad for *Sergeant Deadhead, the Astronut!*, a film Disney released in 1965, in the *Moose Jaw Times Herald*. The movie's initials led him to believe it held the key: SDH. He told everyone Sammy had been banished to the moon. Edmund couldn't wait for any Yankee astronauts to get there and prove him right. The rocket ship he built from propane tanks and an old granary exploded and he was dead long before anyone reached the embers of the fading flames.

The crate in the barn holds all that remains of Sammy Diver Hades and my great uncle's search for him. His writings cover everything from his recollections of Sammy to his pleas for forgiveness to his theories about the forces that took not only Sammy's life away but stole his death as well. There are other artifacts: the ad for *Sergeant Deadhead*, clippings from old encyclopedias, photo albums he had either found at the dump or stolen from a neighbour down the road. There are moments of hope in his records—a boy in one of Edmund's albums is said to be Sammy— but the archive as a whole is confused, illogical, incoherent. The kid in the photos, even a passing glance exposes, couldn't have been born before 1945.

As far as I can tell from the scraps and scribbles, my great uncle had different plans for the material at different times. He was gathering evidence for a trial against the armed forces. Or were they facts for a true history of the Second World War? Near the end it appears he believed a message in a bottle was his only hope, a scroll with Sammy's story contained in glass and blasted onto mountaintops, buried in soils, sands, oceans. Lacking the truth, Edmund longed to find others like himself who believed there was a truth that needed finding.

What have I done? Two things. On the verso of each page you will find transcriptions of my uncle's songs and poems. I have not chosen any of the pieces in which he conjures Sammy, but the pieces where he writes about his personal experience and his imaginings of local legends: rat men, rifles, the building of the old barn (the one, incidentally, my father and I cleaned out). On the recto of each page you will find my attempt to carve out my uncle's little piece of the outside in his illness and paralysis, the work of *art brut* his scraps point to but are too disorganized to compose. I have done my best to tell one of the stories my uncle wanted to tell about Sammy, using the pictures he marked as valuable, the threats he feared, and the apparition he nurtured.

These very different works—my great uncle's extant writings and my rendering of the remains—have been arranged on opposing pages not as a means of putting them into conflict with one another. Nor to make them converse. I did it for those of you who feel like finishing what I have continued. Complete the scroll. Cut these pages from their binding, tape them together and store them rolled in a bottle you toss wherever you best see fit.

Daniel Scott Tysdal
Baildon, SK
(September, 2006)

57

LAST FLIGHT OF SGT DEADHEAD, THE ASTRONUT!

10. THIS JUST IN . . .

Men go missing. They step out for cigarettes. They get in with
the wrong crowd. Some are bandits, others vampires who earn
the stakes that break their hearts in the night. Some are found
buried neck-deep, flesh demolished by ants and sun,
like God planted His raw knuckle in the sand and up grew
a skull. It's in the newspapers. It's all on these ▪, ▪, ▪.

The best of them are heroes. No. Not heroes. The best are not
villains. How'd you like to be cast into an impossible mask
just to prove it's impossible? Ours is such a tale. It's
the story of Sammy Diver Hades. He was sent to kill
the moon. Here he is:

"In
Uniform
and
Posing
with

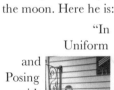

"Side of
House
(in Civvies),
Just
Days Before

Firearm
(During Graduation)"

Lifting
Off"

9. LET'S MURDER THE MOONSHINE

It was the peak of the moon craze. Every nation wanted it DE
Presidents went mad imagining a workforce fortified   AD!
with crumbs of pulverized moon lining their pockets. One king
commissioned a painting of the moon brought down to earth
and carved into a palace for him to master. This dream
of killing the moon was so old, no one could remember the first
sleeper to peep it.

Our Moon Man's Teacher wrote histories of the pursuit.
Once, on the porch of the school, he asked our Sammy,
"What are sea names to a surface that lacks sea spray,
sea birds, the sea?"

BALLAD OF THE MEAN MAN

I read this story once
where the Mean Man made a show
of leavin' the girl who tried
to save him from the glow
of the guns of his pursuers.
He stole her cigarettes
and lit one when they took him down,
said, "I ain't finished yet."

The Mean Man's mean in stealin'.
He's meaner when he gives.
What's alive he wants to die.
What's dead he wants to live.

I read this story once
where the Mean Man finally won.
He finished off the father,
but missed his youngest son.
The boy became a preacher
and wrote that famous prayer:
"God, make dirt the Mean Man's love,
make dust his only heir."

The Mean Man's mean in stealin'.
He's meaner when he gives.
What's alive he wants to die.
What's dead he wants to live.

I read this story once
where the Mean Man made a deal:
for his soul the devil gave him
hands to fully heal
any wound or sickness,
and with these all-curing palms
he lit a stick of dynamite
and held it hard and calm.

The Mean Man's mean in stealin'.
He's meaner when he gives.
What's alive he wants to die.
What's dead he wants to live.

Baildon, 1956

60

8. ON GRADUATION DAY

Five years after enrolling in the first Moon Man Training Program, our Moon Man, Sammy, and his MoonMates were finally ready to murder the moon. Over drinks with cake, they discussed who they were fighting in the name of,

the moon's worst trait,

What it does to our family!

their plans for the future, after the war,

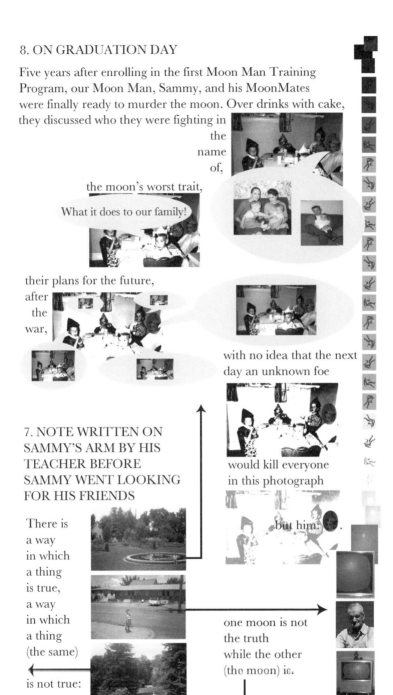

with no idea that the next day an unknown foe

7. NOTE WRITTEN ON SAMMY'S ARM BY HIS TEACHER BEFORE SAMMY WENT LOOKING FOR HIS FRIENDS

would kill everyone in this photograph

but him:

There is a way in which a thing is true, a way in which a thing (the same) is not true:

one moon is not the truth while the other (the moon) is.

BALLAD OF THE RAT MAN

When I was a boy the rats came
and built nests in all we owned:
our barn and bins and tractor,
our coop and cart and home.
My daddy, he tried poisons,
tried water, smoke and hymns.
When that all failed, he said "Ma,
get the Rat Man, Rat Man Jim."

The Rat Man was an old timer,
was built from stone and earth.
His whiskers were cloud-coloured
and growin' since his birth.
He told my brother we could help
by haulin' traps around.
He gave us both tobacco
to spit up on the ground.

The Rat Man said, "These vermin
are really nothin' new.
Did you know that giant rats
killed the King of Timbuktu?"
"Those rats," he said, "were man-sized
and knew how to handle swords.
They had their own arithmetic,
and songs to praise the Lord."

"One breed of rat has reached the moon
and found it full of leaks.
They say its oceans run with dark
and stars wreck all its creeks.
Another breed burrowed beneath
our world's burning core.
Another invented skyscrapers.
Another planned the War."

He said, "The trick to trapping rats
is to understand their dreams.
Its not your right to kill somethin'
until you know just why it screams.
A rat, like you, wants simply life
so you give it life—with a twist.
Think of traps as homes that hold them
for as long as they exist."

All these facts he'd learned from a rat
on the plains right near our Pa's.
The rat told him, "Earth's just God's trap
for keepin' people in his claws."
This rat was a famous outlaw
who robbed banks and torched up land.
Jim told us, "I let him live, though.
How could I kill the real Rat Man?"

Rat Man Jim let our daddy know,
"No payment until the job is done."
He said he'd return in the morning
to clear the traps and set new ones.
Our daddy warned us fairly
after Rat Man Jim was gone
not to listen to half of what Jim said
(not to mention the half that was wrong).

But that night I woke up in the dark
and sneakin' straight outside
I lit a lantern and found a trap
a rat had found then died.
Though his bloodied jaw was clenched,
listening close I could almost feel
him sing the song the Rat Man taught,
"Nibble, nibble. Nibble, nibble. Squeal!"

Baildon, 1959

This is
the nature
of the failure
you will fail to achieve.

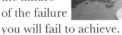

6. OFFICIAL NATIONAL TELE-DISSEMINATOR REPORT ON HIS TEACHER'S CRIME (#7289382)

"This just in,"
the screen beamed.
The screen shone a bad light on
Sammy's Teacher, charging him
with "anti-Anti-Moonism and
disinformationeering." Sammy watched in disbelief
the graphic, animatronic reenactments of the murders
of his MoonMates at the hands of their Teacher. "Our
eyes must dig deep," the screen screamed, "if we are
to truly mine and burn this vile elementBHUUZZ
ZZZZWWWWHRRR!POP!POP!P-"
The screen
repeated: "This just in . . ."

5. FOURTEEN FACTS SAMMY RECORDED FOLLOWING HIS TEACHER'S FINAL VISIT

1) My Teacher killed my friends. 2) He confessed in
my sleeping quarters. 3) My Teacher said: "There is no
Moon. No Mission to kill it." 4) The Mission is: "Fake."
The Mission is: "Not Real." "Moon Men are executed
long before they die the fantastic deaths invented on
the screen." 5) The Mission is: "Conceal This Beast."
6) The calculation he gave me for
This Beast
was:  X
7) Long ago, This Beast plunged into the aquarium and still
it fights for the surface, air, impaling stingray in its jaws,
butchering anemone, starfish, coral. 8) Water clouds.
9) The finger pointing at the Moon absorbs you? 10) Cut it
off 11) Cut off the power of 12) This Power, It lashes
13) life. It shreds fin and face from the lives that can't swim
14) away.

ODE TO A RIFLE

The rifle founds an epic
where the fist just founds a dream
about a hand that fires fingers
in a deadly steady stream.

A baby is an ancient thing.
A stone is something young.
Hunger's in the apple's skin.
Nutrition's in the tongue.

Bullets make two promises:
to kill and uphold peace.
One promise they just make to break,
and one they make to keep.

Baildon, 1960

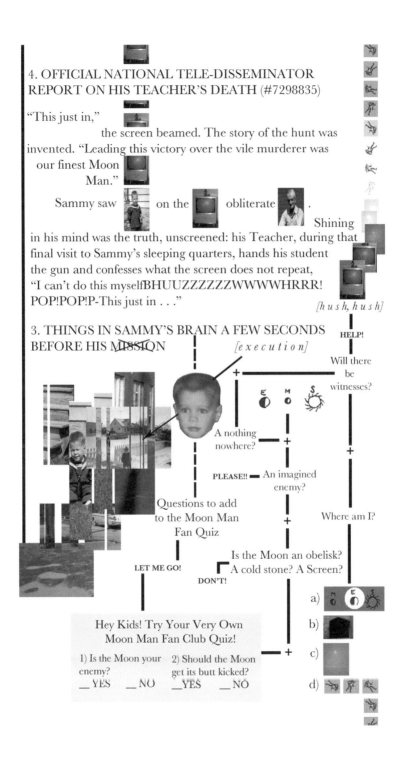

4. OFFICIAL NATIONAL TELE-DISSEMINATOR REPORT ON HIS TEACHER'S DEATH (#7298835)

"This just in,"

the screen beamed. The story of the hunt was invented. "Leading this victory over the vile murderer was our finest Moon Man."

Sammy saw   on the   obliterate   .

Shining in his mind was the truth, unscreened: his Teacher, during that final visit to Sammy's sleeping quarters, hands his student the gun and confesses what the screen does not repeat, "I can't do this myselfBHUUZZZZZZWWWWHRRR! POP!POP!P-This just in . . ."

[h u s h, h u s h]

3. THINGS IN SAMMY'S BRAIN A FEW SECONDS BEFORE HIS ~~MISSION~~

[e x e c u t i o n]

HELP!

Will there be witnesses?

+

A nothing nowhere?

+

PLEASE!! ▬ An imagined enemy?

+

Where am I?

Questions to add to the Moon Man Fan Quiz

+

LET ME GO!

DON'T!

Is the Moon an obelisk? A cold stone? A Screen?

a)

b)

c)

+

d)

Hey Kids! Try Your Very Own Moon Man Fan Club Quiz!

1) Is the Moon your enemy?
___ YES ___ NO

2) Should the Moon get its butt kicked?
___YES ___ NO

65

BALLAD OF THE SHAMED MAN

The shame of being born is bad,
barely beats the shame of death.
None's as bad as the shame of failin'
from breath to breath to breath.
The shame of love is just outdone
by the shame of fear and hate.
The shame of God's not stealin' folks.
It's that He makes them wait and wait.

Shame for what the future brings.
Shame for what it breaks.
Shame for what the past destroys.
Shame for what it fakes.

If shame were up for harvest,
it would yield a whiskey mash.
In fact, I think I tried it once,
a brew like oaken ash.
I danced around a starving mass
and told them, "I'm your saviour."
Think my meal of rocks could teach
the well-fed man's behaviour?

Shame is like that bullet
you aimed to fire through your head.
It caught your mouth and made you howl
for the living not the dead.
Shame is like this cigarette.
It sleeps in its cocoon
and dreams of many-coloured wings
but burns instead and swoons.

The shame of snakes is backwards.
It should be the shame of dirt
for lettin' somethin' evil slither
through its dusty hearth and hurt.
The shame of dirt is upside-down.
It should be the shame of stars
for makin' endless maps in light
that don't lead us very far.

I know I'm meant to sing alone
because skies don't look like ears
and ears don't look like skies with room
for a song ten thousand years
away from bein' finished
though it started with the cry
of the first man to kill his kin
with no good reason why.

Shame for what the future brings.
Shame for what it breaks.
Shame for what the past destroys.
Shame for what it fakes.

Baildon, 1962

2. ON HIS MASTER'S PIPE

The picture-cast-flash
attests to the fact
that pictures are ʳe
 ... ʰot ... ver.
Few are the men
who seek to save men.
Small are the frames
they leave behind to save
what remains.

1. A PILE OF WHAT ARE KNOWN AS PIECES

The people of long ago, a scrap
from our Moon Man's briefings recounts, made up many
stories to explain the pictures they saw in
the moon. "Future myths," his Teacher
foretold, "will be wrought in the reports
of a telecast without end."

The murderers of   our Moon Man,
our Sammy, made   a film about his final
"Mission." **Sergeant DEADHEAD**, they called it, **the AstroNUT!**

On thousands of reels **in PATHECOLOR and PANAVISION**,

AT REGULAR ADMISSIONS, his Rocketmobile's rise
looses a scream one reviewer described as "invention's
failure sounding an original key."

0. OFFICIAL NATIONAL TELE-DISSEMINATOR REPORT ON THE RECOVERY OF HIS CORPSE (#7300590)

This just in

ODE TO A BARN

The first memory I recall
is watchin' this barn rise
into a sky where nothin' stood,
the nothin' there said, "Bye."

What if endless fires raged
and swept the barns away?
Where would we keep our tools and toil?
Where would the critters stray?

The first memory I recall
is of our dog chasin' a fox.
My father raised his rifle, aimed.
Guess which one he shot.

Baildon, 1951

Interlude

PLEASE ACCEPT MY CONDO

Her cell phone cut my deepest sympathies
short. The fault of a patchy connection, she guessed,
when she showed me days later and we laughed off
our faces at my truncated text. I didn't know her
adequately to ask who she'd lost; we were barely
close enough to suffer a telecommunicational blip.
"Please accept my condo" was all that had not
been swallowed by the gaps the sky works
into an ether between towers, as though solace
were the embrace of a room so new you were
certain no one had died in its thoughtless hold.
Or maybe the defective note was meant for me;
I needed to make real the imperative of that
half-sentence and tell this woman in her grief
to care for my concrete cocoon, while I emerged for her
as a mourning cloak butterfly, of the family *nymphalis*,
so weightless in those winds I was the drunk
who bobbed without sense on the ocean-filled waterbed
of the earth, no path too straight for me to fail it.
Future phones should be programmed to make new
our tongues. "We must honour the memo"
will be our promise to the bereaved, and to dads
and moms freshly minted we'll cry: "Congratulations
on the birth of yo." So novelly mobile,
so strangely celled, we will be as original
as the back-flipping dog who learned to leave
his trick unfinished and dangle, flea-bitten, in the air.

Breaking News

The latest news from Kandahar is that the sounds of war have changed. Or so Private Nathan Thomas Hales told his wife in the last email he sent from Afghanistan. Years ago a great uncle had returned from Europe shocked by the thundering of heavy artillery, and one of the Private's earliest memories was of witnessing this man's immensity collapse at the sound of a backfiring engine. What would make him collapse, Hales wondered, when he returned home? A smoothly running engine was his best guess. The sounds of combat were now the sounds of travel. The hum of an engine carried you to roadside explosives. It was the sound that sent a car your way, the trunk packed with five hundred pounds of fire. The guys who lose it, Private Hales had been warned, were those who couldn't quit asking themselves with each approaching car, with each paved mile: Is this the one? Because that question soon gave way to the knowledge that it's this one, this one, no, this one, until you made it back safe or finally got it.

The first soldiers to receive news of the Private's death were those injured with him in the blast, then those in the convoy's surrounding vehicles, including the freelance journalist who caught the explosion on tape, preserving the blast and the smoke-shredded metal smouldering in the road. His bunkmates at the base learned next, his tablemates, the guy in supplies who got the wrong face in his head and when he saw the man he thought had died went weak in the knees. One of the first civilians to receive the news was Private Hales's wife, Maria. After the call, she closed the bedroom door on her sleeping child and watched her brother play an army-filled video game she had never understood: too many buttons, the controls just too complex. A week before he died, Nathan had asked their son to start meeting him in his dreams. That night Maria dreamed of a bridge with haunted trains, a marble staircase that led only to more stairs, towering smoke stacks.

In each of her dreams she was alone. And she woke alone the next morning, heaved from sleep by another call from one of the documentarians working on a film titled, *Back Home: The Lives Soldiers Leave Behind*. The documentarian gave his condolences and asked if he could speak with her after finishing up at the farm where Nathan was raised. He would understand if she said no. When they had arrived to continue filming, Maria's father-in-law had simply hollered at them from the house to get what they needed but leave him be. The documentarians were there to re-shoot footage of an old school bus Nathan's father had converted into a motor home. When Nathan was a boy, his father had wanted to take his son to see Canada's four corners but the thing had broken down after one trip to the west coast. It was now populated by trapped moths and mice, and knickknacks Nathan had picked up in South Korea while training with the Americans. When one of the documentarians returned to town to meet with Maria, the other remained in the bus and smoked a joint. He shot portraits of the flag he found. Eyed the patterns of window-pinned flies. He paired a dead mouse with different artifacts but, well into the process, looking over the footage, he couldn't remember why.

The stoned documentarian was eventually dragged from the bus and sent stumbling back to town through acres of stubble and snow. Nathan's father gave him the boot after hearing 680 Talk Radio's Renegade Randy describe the ramp ceremony as another punch line in this joke of a war. He wanted it gone, he thought, grabbing his shotgun from the closet, everything not contained by the distance his eye could see into the surrounding yard. But what could he really target? The radio host? The documentarians? The animals he could watch starve as he starved himself? There was all the chatter of the telephone to stop. All the chatter of the television, the World Wide Web. Just cross the country on foot, was his advice to himself, and bring a little quiet back to things, room by room, home by home.

Half a planet between them, Nathan's father levelled the barrel of his rifle at the men overseas. The ones who built the thing that killed his son. In his heart he felt he knew them. What they waited on and feared. He aimed at them, at all that was hateful in their works and words. He aimed back in time as the day grew dark, back before they had built their explosive, before they were born, even, he aimed way back before any of these mothers birthed sons and he waited for a blast that would sound away everything but now, now, now, and, passing, now. He waited in the cold all night. He waited to hear that he'd got them.

But no such news came. Preparations continued in Nathan's hometown of Moose Jaw in anticipation of his return. Mayor Dale McBain couldn't decide where to hold the press conference announcing his plan to dedicate a park to the city's fallen son. His advisors were divided between a war memorial, the armouries, and the mock-up of a trench the city had funded at a local museum. Mr. Walter Everett, principal of A. E. Peacock Collegiate, wanted someone to tell him it was right to build a statue for his former student alongside the metal figures of Winston Churchill and the Man of Industry. One chatty transient, a man known only as Acid Bob, told a stranger he was improvising a memorial for Nathan and then pointed to a flock of departing birds.

The future prepared for the body as well. The light and shadows taking the place of another life unlived. The minds of the living playing the lost life out for it. In a few hours, Nathan's father will begin work on a homemade coffin for his son that the funeral home will talk him out of using. It will remain stored in the barn among the rest of the debris—gravel, seized machines, a homemade ventriloquist dummy his grandson had been too scared to hold—until his own death, leaving those who survive him to dispose of it all in his absence. In the decades ahead a descendent will write a report on her Great Grandfather Nathan, the defender of freedom. A future historian will miss Nathan's body in his tally of bodies but will still manage to articulate the breadth of the losses. The sun will one day dim, or grow even more fiery and explode, and take with it all the roads, the trapped animals, the billowing in our dreams.

But none of this will happen before Martin Joseph, a freelance journalist returning home from Afghanistan, decides what to do with the footage he shot of Private Nathan's dying moments. Joseph had kept the footage a secret, concealing his camera on his person at all times as he travelled from the blast to the base, from the base to the airport terminal, from the terminal to the plane. No one would know until he decided. Disseminate or delete? He had been hunkered far from where the blast had thrown the body but the lens had made him intimate with the tones of burns and bleeding, the last-worded quivering of colour-sapped skin. He would watch the tape one more time. One more look was all he needed. Before the plane landed in its clamour of turbines and tires he would know exactly what to do.

dew

with Special thanks to Daniel S. Tysdal for his notebooks (1992-1999)

The world of dew
is a world of dew
And yet   and yet
                    Issa

This is how it ends°, almost; 16, spring
of '94, a child composes not
in some obscure Morse code°, not with the walls
of a haiku. He writes plain phrases: "kill
myself°," "To whoever it may concern°,"   5
each cartoon bubble with cartoon° letters
reading "the end°." It is time°. It is time
to take the hand° of the long departed,
or the wrist of one with self-inflicted
scars like too many spectres° too many   10
spectators° staring condemn. It is time
to tempt Duk Koo Kim's° cry "Kill or be killed°"
and re-orchestrate the composition
known as I°: bend down over the barrel
of the rifle as though pouring the self   15
in and wait, cocked, to find when fired the blank
patches of the atmosphere°, the sleep white
and cold°. Browing wrote, 'What youth deemed crystal,
Age finds out was dew. Now° nearly 30,
in the autumn of '07, I show   20

Editor's Note: The degree sign (o) indicates a footnote, which is keyed to the
text by the line number; the source follows handwritten. 1 This is how it ends
3 obscure Morse code 4 kill myself 5 To whoever it may concern
6 cartoon bubble w/ cartoon 7 the end: It is time 8 hand 10 too many specters
10 11 too many spectators 12 Duk Koo Kim: "Kill or be killed" 13-14 the composition known as I
17 empty patches of the atmosphere 17-18 asleep white and cold (sup?) 19 Now

my friend the page I wrote that day, amazed
at such certainty. She jots down Browning's
couplet. She's right: the crystal that entombed me,
that shining guided me to write this

page

does evaporate, does dim, but crystal—   25
what was it in the first place, even° then°,
if not dew stone-hardened devouring dew?

These leftovers of an empire° once great
in the grace° of ▨▨▨▨, these genuine journals,
they seem to save on each actual page   30
from an actual notebook° /one [those
sketched. The mind remembering, it mirrors°
a mirror°. Nerves shiver under the shapes
of the past, the buried moods intruding,
how it once felt to write "It is I," "me,"   35
"It's me." This is° how it felt to be young°
and believe "To whoever it may concern"
was the right toast for the many mournings°
I almost invited to wake. Youth's all
is an aperture unable to glimpse   40
the companions who pictured the future
the same—as nothing°, nothing°, no. Like dew°
their hands condensed in my notebooks:
a lock of ▬▬▬ , a ✿ , a ♡ — ¿ — in the abyss
of before that did not shine. Kerouac's°   45
"Light fades, I pass,°" was appended by now,
pass° now°. Building the town that binds° meant "find
a cure° in drink°, pills°, and medication°,

26 even; Then 28 Leftovers of an Empire; due grch 29 Grace 31 actual page from
32 mirrors 33 a mirror 36 this is; be young 38 Many Mournings
42 nothings; nothing; dew 45 Kerouac 46 "Light fades, I pass,"
47 pass; Now; town that binds us 48 find a cure;
drink; pills; medication

self-induced nightmares° and acid trip° myths
recounted from the bathroom floor°." Yeah, yeah,   50
this story's condensed, flattened a little.
There was some *~~love~~*, and *Love* °
*ya*s and *i love you*s°.
But these marks were faulty as songs without
melodies at making memorable loss,
the *mori* of the *memento mori*   55
my companions inked and compelled:

DROP FOR LIFE °
,

Keep drinking; °

PARTY TILL YA DIE '!!! °

3.1

"*Thems days have come and gone* "°, my grandfather
observed. I transcribed, crossing some crosswalk
in Moose Jaw I helped his 3-legged evening   60
traverse, some time, some season in nineteen-
ninety-three. Are *Thems days*° like dew after
an apocalypse without branches *come*°
and gone°? Or do they remain like the dew
whose droplets travel unbroken from leaf   65
to stream to cloud and back to leaves with each
downpour? The answers in my notebook scrap:
one page claims *yesterday and tommorow*
will be One°, another rewrites Shakespeare's
epitaph for his star-crossed kids as "*all*   70
are reconciled°" without changing the fate
of the "punish'd," extracting mortal drugs,
or making breasts again from sheaths. The old
Zen algorithm° calculates it best:

49 *self induced nightmares*; *acid trip* 50 *the bathroom floor*
52 Love ya; i love you 56 DROP FOR LIFE 57 keep drinking;
PARTY TILL YA DIE! 58 "Thems days have come and gone"
62 Thems days 63 come 64 and gone 66-69 yesterday and tommorow
will be One 70-71 all are reconciled 74 *Zen algorithm*

Thems days° are here and gone°, come° and yet to   75
commence—changing: All is one

one is none

none is all°. The flood still rises. If once
the lament went that no one built an ark°,
know now the flood itself is so many
arks dashed against arks that the saviour
will be rain—or the sky°, or stone°, or fire°,   80
whatever finally falls and resolves
which vessel best assails which path, which song
of voices° to coax which crew, which lifetime
hidden° among the millions and millions
inside these pages is the best to give   85
a ten-count in reverse before crying,
"Ready or not. Here I° come°."

4

If the note book° were the world there would be
no final draft°. Erasing my granddad's
"Thems days°" would restore his lines to extend   90
well beyond their unlasting lengths. Or take
the faith-fixing mistakes in every prayer
to promise paradise with handmade blasts.
If the world were a note book° we could ink
amid the margins of their knelling, & NEEDS   95
LOTS OF WORK°; we could pen "change°" atop saints
who avenge in obliterating hues
the shades that make hazy their ruling howl
(inverting some silly Romantic's° hope
from two centuries ago), "What we hated,   100
others will hate, and we will teach them how."
The truth is the note book° is the notebook,
the world the world, and creeping into Seung

75 Thems days; gone; come 76 "All is one / one is none / none is all"
77 no one built an ark 80 sky; stone; fire 82-83 Song of Voices
83-84 lifetime hidden 87 Here I; come 88 note book 89 final draft
90 Thems days 94 note book 95-96 * NEEDS LOTS OF WORK
96 change 99 silly little romantic 102 note book

Hui Cho's dorm months before "Virginia Tech,"
reworking his manifestoes and plays   105
into sympathetic cries—a sound poem
to out-crescendo the empty orchestra
of his vitriol—wouldn't change a thing.
He'd return, and return his abhorrence
to its syllabic patter. No phrases   110
could snap him into seeing the self forged
into a photo, through which one cold face
makes ash of all that is not its loathing
staring out from the frame (at its loathing
staring in), as the self erased; the I   115
expires if all expressions are death masks
smashed before they're cast. The dew we gather
could never dampen such a willful thirst.
So, like Dylan Thomas wrote, gather what
you can, "hear the dew falling, the hushed town   120
breathing, and with *your* eyes unclosed" study
the palmed pressure Professor Librescu
submitted to that door, that direction
he decided in an instant to rush.
He faced Cho's fury. His students escaped.   125
The signature of this survival must
be written down. What's the word for the peace
greeted in that farewell Donne bid the slave
of Fate and desperate kings? Look how, centuries
later, it was re-cast so swollen, dumb,   130
hackneyed, and pale in this adolescent
scrawl: Death Death Death Death
Death Death Death Death
Death Death Death Death° die.

This is how it ends°. We return these drafts
and notebooks to their homes: closets, basements,
garages, crates, barns dusted with the waste   135
of birds. We kiss goodnight for good the work
we planned to, but will not finish later°,

132 Death (x12) 133 This is how it ends 137 finish later

the rhyme that's an epic and ends CUT TO:
Black and some kind of music°, the list words
are winged in, escaping for a ~they fall   140
short of even without us. All that's left
is to crest the peaks of our strokes and gaps
with an epigraph that utters their vigour,
crystallizes the hope they will make _hope_°
held. How about this one haiku Issa   145
composed centuries ago? Over centuries,
it was translated, transformed, fouled and failed,
passed on and lauded; many surfaces
were marked with those syllables we first heard—
if for right now you pretend we were me—   150
when our friend on the streetcar drew closer
and exhaled a world of dew in our ear
with the promise, later, to write it down.

138-139 _CuT To Black. And some kind of mux_ 144 hope

Interlude

THE HISTORIANS ARE DEAD

No one knows or knew. The Drano
of their deaths wiped clean the pipes
and in that wipe the pipes went, too.

"The platforms for the dead are all they love,"
the gladdened said, though don't remember
saying, "Fill subway trains with the present
dead, the dead made present, and historians
will complain!"

Others lamented, before forgetting their own
lament, that none would ever know what trains
once travelled, or were, or bore, when the thing
we build to replace the train arrives to carry
what trains had borne to burn or bury.

One year has passed, or no time at all
(or has it been three centuries?), since the papers
said in screaming fonts the historians
have left us, and that if our dead alone
are them, then we're the dead with none
to know or note it.

The Open Toll

EULOGY FOR BLAIR
written for Blair Desi Smith (July 18, 1978–January 12, 2009)

Dear Blair,

My favourite memories are of you and me creating.

I remember the short movies we made in high school. While filming the fight scene for *Plastic Face 4*, I remember how you accidentally knocked me silly, leaving a goose egg on my forehead the size of a golf ball. I remember cresting the hill on my dad's old riding lawnmower, you at the wheel and me standing tall on the seat behind you, the two of us hollering "Ride of the Valkyries" at the top of our lungs, while we shot the forgotten blockbuster, *Billy Bobcat and Andy Apocalypse Meet the Turkey King.*

I remember all the conversations over coffee and tea in the years after high school, planning the next big project—the movie, the play, the album—whatever it was we never quite got around to finishing, too caught up in the fun of what we *could do* to be worried about what we actually got done.

Most of all, Blair, I remember the songs we sang together. Or, I should say, the songs I sang while you played your guitar. I remember never being able to get you to sing. Where I heard a gruffer Tom Waits in your vocals, you must have heard something like a garburator chomping on a jet engine. You seemed to think you sang that poorly.

I remember practising our favourites late into the night—REM, Johnny Cash and, of course, Dave Matthews—until your hand finally cramped up so bad you could barely open it. I remember performing in Crescent Park for whoever passed by. I remember busking on Main. I remember we recorded a tape before I left for South Korea. It's what I listened to whenever I felt so far from home.

The qualities that made you a great partner in art, Blair, are what made you a great friend.

I will miss your generosity. I will miss your very vocal love for your family and friends. I will miss those moments you would let go and be joyous. I will miss that joy's outcome: your oh so distinct Blair laugh. I will miss hearing you call me "Danny Boy."

I will miss your sensitivity to the suffering of others. I remember seeing you after a shift at Bugsy's. A table of drunks had mockingly impersonated a departing patron's disability. You were so furious and sad you were shaking. I will miss your expressions of anger at injustice, at what you knew wasn't fair, those moments where most people would just brush the pain of someone else aside and say, "So?"

I never thought I'd say this, Blair, but I will miss your stubbornness (even if sometimes it meant you would try and argue a blue sky into believing it was green). I think it was your stubbornness, your refusal to believe you had done enough, your refusal to accept that this is how the world had to be, that made your generosity and your compassion so endless.

The question is the same for all of us now.

Why?

We ask why we didn't do more to help you. We ask why we failed you. We ask ourselves why we were where we were when it happened. Why wasn't I there to take your hand and say, "No"?

But knowing you, Blair, hearing these questions makes you want to be the one who takes our hands and says, "Don't." You want to say, "No more 'Whys'." You want to keep us from the pain of loss and blame. You were in "a world of hurt," as you would put it, and you did not want anyone else to suffer there.

You made a world of good, too, though, Blair, for those of us around you. You did this with your creativity and sense of humour, with the energy of your presence and the uniqueness of your personality. You did this with your belief in our talents and your hopes for our futures.

The one "Why" I will never let go, Blair, no matter how much you would want me to, is this: Why didn't you let yourself into this better world? Why didn't you extend more of your generosity and your kindness to yourself?

I wish you had.

I wish there could be one more song. I wish I could feel the weight of your guitar in my hand as I passed it to you. I wish, as you started strumming, I could say, "Blair, sing with me. Sing. Sing. Sing. Sing." Even if you didn't join me in the melody, I'd keep pushing. I'd get you laughing. That's how we'd begin.

Yours with love and thanks and the deepest regrets,

Danny Boy

Hic Jacet

CALL

Dear Mr. Daniel Scott Tysdal:

Good day to you. My name is Jim Franklin. I am writing from sunny Yellow-knife. I used to run a rod and gun shop up here, but I'm retired now and make my residence in North River. I'm in Yellowknife right now to take what they call a "continuing education" course, and to visit with my son who runs the old store (if you'd like to see the shiny new website you can click here). I'm not one for pleasantries, so if you don't mind, I'll get right to it. I need your help.

Just yesterday, in that class I was telling you about, I saw this painting of a hanged woman done by a German fellow named Richter. The woman, we learned, was Gudrun Ensslin and the painting was a part of a show called, *October 18, 1977*. The paintings for this series were made from photographs that documented the events surrounding what was either the collective suicide or extrajudicial execution of five jailed members of a German left-wing terrorist organization called the Baader-Meinhof Gang. At the time she died in her cell, this woman, Ensslin, had been in police custody for five years, much of it spent in solitary confinement. Terrible, yes, but that's not what shocked me.

Later on that same day, I sat down at my grandson's computer to post a new poem on my blog (like you I'm a "burgeoning bard" (if you're curious click this)). There was a web browser open. The screen was filled with the filthiest words and pictures I've ever seen. The Internet's arsehole would be putting it nice. I was about to close the browser when a word that didn't fit with the rest of the foulness caught my eye: "POPEYE." The sailor? The spinach-muncher? The anchor-tattooed? I couldn't help clicking the thing to see the new page.

The woman's name was not given. The bus that had taken her life gave no clue to the where or when or why of her death. There was nothing about the events of her life before it, the passage of her body. Her eye. That was the whole thing. She was pinned under the name of a goddamned cartoon sailor, framed by porn ads and links to only God knows what.

I wrote a poem, "Monument" (which you'll find attached). When that didn't change the way I was reeling, I decided to write to poets who I thought might be able to help. Lucky you. You're one of them. No real question other than: what the hell do you make of this?

With the hope of hearing from you soon,
J.G. Franklin

RESPONSE

Gudrun Ensslin (15.8.40–18.10.77):
Member of the Baader-Meinhof
Gang (found hanged in her cell by her
own hand or the hands of guards).
Revolutionary Anarchist Violent
Criminal. Sworn enemy of Yankee
hegemony and German author-
itarianism. Leader in the war of 6
against 60 million. Anti-fascist
terrorist and martyr monster (an-
cestors repudiated Hitler). One of
History's chosen, accidentally or
otherwise.

[The Anonymous
Woman] (????-????):
Tire tread streaked
onto street and traffic
lined up behind bus,
behind the accident,
behind her. Her. No
name or nation on
pavement, motion-
flattened skull-lessness
for this online afterlife
and a respite from
the socket for the eye
popped free.

Hi Mr. Franklin,

Thank you for sharing this: these images, your shock,
your poem. I hope I can help.

I have started something. I'm not sure what. An attempt
at burial? An attempt to make her part of a different
chorus? I'll send the poem to you when I'm done.

"Hic Jacet" is the working title. That means: Here Lies.

With best regards,
Daniel

POPEYE

but she

can't see

why (her

eye,

bulging

her eye,

blind)

CUT

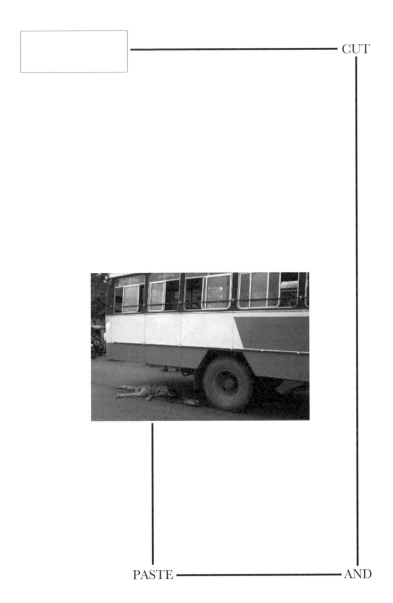

PASTE ——————————— AND

UBI EST?
Submission #37 (Adhita Dasgupta / Victoria, BC)

In this dance the dead lead, the dead
are the only dancers
dancing. And in the triumph of Death
over those who head
His procession and those
who falling under
follow, Death is drawn
by dumb beasts who draw wheels
that impress His path on

and on. But where her feet
lose hold beneath His carriage's slow
roll forth is not so certain. Or how
in that dancing her footprints fall, then
fall, is nowhere disclosed in the dancing's

ascent. If prayers are pilgrims
for unborn births, then here
is a prayer for whatever remains unborn
in all that will never be born
again. Here is a pilgrimage
that begins by asking where is

she among the anonymous
graves that locals hoped to mark
with names long-sealed in buried
records? Or on that stream
the tour guide claimed
ghost soldiers float in search of

home, where is she along
their waveless trails, their vacant
vessels in an invisible repose we travellers
were told to close our eyes before
and kneel?

PLANE

Instructions for Form Letter

1. Cut out letter and sign name on line provided.

2. Fold letter in half.

3. Using the dotted lines , fold down front corners to base of first fold.

4. Fold again to base.

5. Repeat.

6. Hold centre and open wings.

7. Throw hard enough to reach her (but not so hard that it never leaves the sky).

CUT

CUT

Dear Gudrun,

I am writing with a request on behalf of a friend. He saw a painting of you made from a photo (not one of the shots of you caught by surprise as you left (or returned to) your cell, but the one where you remain there, hanging). He needs you—your revolutionary expertise and anger at an age—to look into an album he's compiling. There's an image of an anonymous woman struck down by a bus that ended up desecrated online. How can he detonate the name that disdains her? How do you shape a new grave?

Though he cannot read or speak your tongue, he's learned a few words (*expressionismus*, for example, *am ende*); and though he claims your politics would've forced you to despise his work, here's to hoping there's a link between his dream of a word-traced revolution without hijacking or terror and your hope, unspoken but implicit in your deeds, that the elegizing that overtook prophecy and revelation will itself finally die.

Please respond if possible.

Yours,

_____

CUT

MONUMENT
Submission #1 (J.G. Franklin / North River, NWT)

There are only a few lumps of clay for this monument,
a little grey to grow her, all the hands that held a hand
in her demise, its perseverance. Her hands as they are

in the photographer's. Or as they were, maybe clenched,
maybe raised and hailing a cab. With so little clay,
from the fingers at the wheel that failed to swerve
must grow the nails that scraped the pavement clear of
her blood. Each hand you sculpt begets one
hundred hands, the impermanence of each unfired pair
affirmed for the sake of the next impermanent

set. And you wonder while kneading away the most
meticulously sculpted wrinkles and half-surfacing veins,
while erasing the space at the edge of a crafted wrist
where a forearm, implied, resided,
whether there's a monument erectable in the name
of all these failed monuments, whether there's a map
to shake dirt from and follow to some robust continent
amid whose animals and clear mists might arise
a whole terrain of hands sculpted in the honour of

destroyed sculpted hands. You wonder why even though
you aim each time for a clay replica of the earth, the ultimate
quarry, built to scale, you end again and again with
your own hands sculpting your own hands, four malleable palms
to leave pressed in the grass in the impossible promise to build

for what gets buried without disturbing all that already lies buried
amid the abandoned burrows, cracked seeds, and tunnels
winding silent round irrecoverable roots that no longer bear life
beyond the surface of the soil's lone breach.

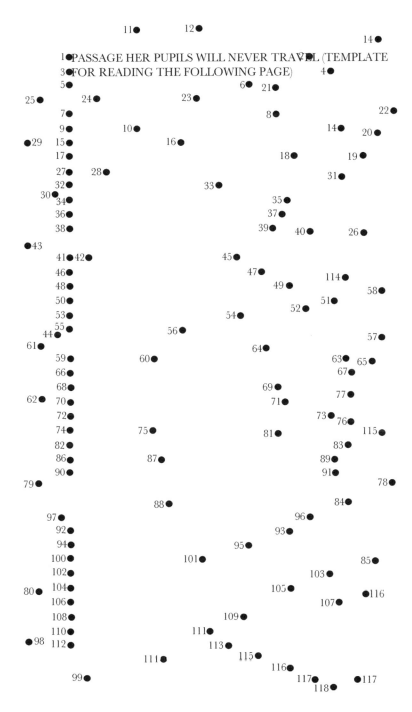

PASSAGE HER PUPILS WILL NEVER TRAVEL (TEMPLATE
FOR READING THE FOLLOWING PAGE)

Gudrun Ensslin (15.8.40-18.10.77): Member of the Baader-Meinhof Gang. (For more flip back six pages.)

A Memento Mori For When the Dead Are the Props that Really Get the Troops and the Laughtrack Fired Up

Submission #4 (Daniel Scott Tysdal / Toronto, ON)

[The Anonymous Woman] (????-????): Tire tread streaked onto street. (For more close your eyes, flip.)

I read that you understood *Measure for Measure*
and *Moby Dick*, Gudrun—the copies of these works you kept
in your cell—as allegories
for the revolution. And I see you seeing this image—
either as founding some symmetry (which translates as *ebenmaß*)
between a woman's skull caved in
by a bus (crowded online with other "demented (*wahnsinnig,*
shit"[1]) and the immense, machinic musculature in your language,
of that progress you had hoped to murder, or *scheiße*)

re: when the mani-festo dis-places mourning.

as a chance to seize the chance to cite
yourself, to bark what you barked at rallies
about "[v]iolence [being] the only way to answer
violence,"[2] insinuating that to answer the violence of death
with violence exacted against the dead (*die gewalt*)
makes sense, and this image posted

re: when death is the oppposite of a change in the whole sensorium, as one body of knots and alone oblivionates

(in your tongue *expressionismus,*
under the name Popeye rightfully calls up words like abstract, *abstrakter*)
or expression, because the colouration, the patterning of brain
on road, is scented slightly like certain spatters
paint made during the rigor mortis of obedience
and beauty; windmilling arms, in their videotaped plunge
from burning, towered heights, are meant (*bedeuten*)
to be laughed at alongside grainy footage of the earliest attempts
at flight; and, in the end, the only real downer about dying
is that we'll miss the punchline our dying inspires. No need

(am ende)

Those triple-decker contraptions that barely betrayed gravity before splintering barns to bits.

to worry about what your opponent said to quiet
the controversy surrounding your burial:—
"All enmity should cease after
death."[3] All enmity will not, Gudrun, I know, and maybe
for a moment we can't even imagine formulating
a form that sees it otherwise, in which one life's experiences
silenced in their spread beneath transit
end up as something other than
that nickname [I mentioned earlier] (*knall auge,* for you)

but she can't see why (her eye, bulging her eye, blind)

(in the same grave as two allies who had died in the same shared imprisonment)

90

PASSAGES BURIED ON THE PREVIOUS PAGE

PASSAGE GUDRUN MOST LIKELY UNDERLINED IN *MOBY DICK*

"Glimpses do ye seem to see of that mortally intolerable truth; that all deep, earnest thinking is but the intrepid effort of the soul to keep the open independence of her sea; while the wildest winds of heaven and earth conspire to cast her on the treacherous, slavish shore? But as in landlessness alone resides highest truth, shoreless indefinite as God—so better is it to perish in that howling infinite, than be ingloriously dashed upon the lee, even if that were safety!"

BURIAL PRACTICE THE POET FAILED TO ADDRESS

Of the many traditions lost with this people's disappearance, perhaps the most unique is their practice of fashioning a doll—a single, silent palm-sized avatar of the deceased—from the remains of the deceased. Slices of tanned skin form the bodies of the extant examples, and stuffed with powdered bone they continue to hold their shape. The expressions of the faces are composed, in all cases, from carved teeth. The dolls were meant to mark, most experts agree, the site where the life was lost, and the dolls may have acted as vehicles for lost or avenging souls, or as reminders of things to come. What makes this practice truly unique, though, are the skirts and robes that clothe the dolls. DNA analysis of these articles revealed that the clothes, stitched from human skin, are not stitched from the skin of the deceased. The skin comes from elsewhere. Experts have speculated that this flesh originated with everyone from dead kin to slave babies sacrificed to serve as the purist attire. Others imagine the skin was given by the doll's maker, a part of themelves handed over to protect what they will not let go.

PASSAGE GUDRUN MOST LIKELY UNDERLINED IN *MEASURE FOR MEASURE*

"He should have lived, / Save that his riotous youth with dangerous sense / Might in times to come have ta'en revenge / By so receiving a dishonoured life / With ransom of such shame."

BURIAL PRACTICE THE POET FAILED TO ADDRESS

What makes the Living Gardens Cemetery unique is that the deceased are not buried in their plots. Instead, they occupy for eternity the earth they would have traditionally been thrown under. Thanks to Living Gardens' two-fold preservation process, which involves plastinating the corpse's exterior and animating the skeletal structure with cutting-edge robotics technology, the deceased are not only saved from decomposition, but they can at once endure a whole range of climates and physically interact with their mourners (a rigorous maintenance regime and daily exercises keep the dead fresh and limber). Living Gardens currently has more than 200 inhabitants and following the mass disappearance in the fall of 2022—when the resident dead were either stolen or malfunctioning, wandered off—there have been no escapees or departures.

PASSAGE FROM HER NAMESAKE

"I am what I am."

excerpt from ELE-G
Submission #105 (YEAH!ts / Halifax, NS)

There are no Godfathers among poets, only Fredos,
on the lake with our killer with no way to lay low.
They're Play-Doh soft, the prayers we say so
Mother Mary full of grace will—Wait!
Elegy is the road most crept by those who don't move,
the step untaken that untaken leaves mountains lept,
miles moved, mountains grooved
with the faces of the Gods of All Stasis who settled
for earth when they couldn't reach the moon.
A word that means every word is: Terminal.
A sickness with a limit is: Germinal.
A urinal's a unicorn. A unicorn's a kernel
of the poppity-popcorn they won't serve in the theatre
      at the eye of the storm.
The history of elegy is the misery of going free
in a language that's a prison—aw, shit, prisons grow on trees.
The mystery of elegy is it's the game's only play
when the clock's countin' down, the crowd's gone away,
the crowd's gone away, the clock's countin' down,
silence fouled out and your opponent's all sound.

Call for Submissions

On behalf of J.G. Franklin, we would like to announce an open call for poems of any size and duration. The works should make a new resting place for the Anonymous Woman. Name or reclaim or question or sustain where she rests with any tongue-fluttering sounds and syntactical arrays. Fidelity to the task is the only stimulation. How, for example, can we detonate the fixity of the range that engrains her? How can we escape the same grave?

The editor will also consider works that think through the Anonymous Woman's relationship to any fellow travellers, sister saints, or enemies of her state. For example, in the case of Richter's Gudrun Ensslin, how do these two women embody the extreme final routes progress unburies for its annihilatable elements (the extreme degrees different gears reach to whisk skin silent)? How are they buoyed or betrayed by the fundamental modes of preservation—the museum with walls and the one without—that progress sustains?

Please send all submissions with an SASE to:

J.G. Franklin, Editor
Hic Jacet
Box 143
North River, NWT
X0E 0L0

Deadline: ∞

CRANE

1. Cut

2. Fold:

3. Place out
of doors.

4. Wait

5. for breeze

6. or the motion

7. of the open

8. infinity

9. of the waves

10. of the sea.

CAIRN

CAIRN

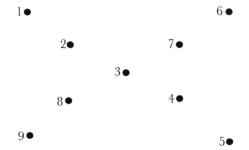

CAIRN

ALBUMS THAT AWAIT YOUR REPLY

Interlude

THE CHAIR

We can't help
but see a face: "LOL Chair," it's affectionately called
online. Two screws form the eyes. The grin
is the gap in the chair's metal back. With the news
that our government has ceased to sit, just try not to see
our great leader's face in the face in the chair.
Turn the gap in the back upside down, add the nose,
and you've got him:

Plato would lose it: a chair—already so far removed
in ink from its ideal form—degraded by the addition
of the features of a ruler satirized for ruling. "Look
at the poets," he'd state, "validating your right
to prorogue. For them? What's the good? They find
your face in a chair without realizing they can't even
see you. You're a true leader, Harper, your true
features at all cost remain hidden."

Then what does Stephen see? When he sees us
from his seclusion? What is it in the lines of our faces
that make us so impossible to represent? Maybe he's
the poet, and in place of our features he finds this:　,
a slot with two screws at the threshold of an entrance
in which the lock of the door as it closes catches and holds

Every Voice Matters /
These Angels Taken

In the summer of 2007, Canada Post announced the "Every Voice Matters" campaign, its plan to sponsor a memorial to commemorate the one-year anniversary of the Dawson College shootings. The announcement was made in a two-page ad that appeared in the Saturday, June 30th, editions of the *Toronto Star, Globe and Mail,* and *Le Journal de Montréal.*

The campaign announcement consisted of three sections. On the recto side of the page was the advertisement composed simply of three lines: "Patrice Tousignant remembers hearing the shots and the friend who saved her. / What do you remember? / Every Voice Matters." The ad appeared throughout the summer on billboards and buses, on the radio and TV. The last two lines remained the same in each. Only the person and the memory changed.

On the verso side of the campaign announcement a letter from Canada Post President and CEO Moya Greene, explained the goals. The memorial was to be assembled in Dawson College cafeteria on September 13th and composed of contributions from "people like you who wish to remember." After a one-week stay, the memorial would be donated to the National Gallery in Ottawa. "When it comes to never forgetting these angels who are taken too soon," she wrote in closing, "every voice matters."

The most important element of the announcement was the two-inch strip along the edge of the paper set off by a dotted vertical line. On the strip's recto, the paper was blank. On the verso a Montreal address was printed along with a stamp that read, "Postage Paid if Mailed in Canada." Though contributors were welcome to send whatever object of remembrance they desired (a personal painting, a stuffed animal (flowers were discouraged)), Moya Greene suggested they make use of the free strip. Fill the blank space, cut it free from the ad, and drop it in the mail. For those who missed the original ad, the form could be downloaded online and printed up at home. The deadline for inclusion in the memorial was August 31st.

Every Saturday leading up to the event, *Globe and Mail* published an exclusive article detailing the piece a famous Canadian was creating for the campaign. The message from opposition leader Stéphane Dion. The original composition by R. Murray Shafer. Filmmaker Atom Egoyan looped the security footage of Gill's entrance and ran it in reverse so that "Gill does what we want, he leaves, but the nature of the loop brings us, brings him, back to reality." Egoyan planned to transfer the tape to a more mail-able strip of 35mm film. For her piece, "Going Postal," Nicole Brossard covered the page in black, writing over and over again the phrase from Kimveer's blog she said most disturbed her, "Life is a videogame and you gonna die sometime."

Taking off from Greene's comment about angels and voice, the following poem was my contribution. It needed strips from three newspapers to complete. Though I sent them together, on the same day, there was no way of assuring they ended up joined.

Daniel Scott Tysdal
Toronto, ON
(September 2007)

THESE ANGELS TAKEN

*Every angel
is terrifying.*
            —Rilke

1.

Even the absence
of angels in
the story by the girl
who quit her creative
writing class, the story
she offered "about
a woman with nowhere
to go." A baby
dies in an alley, alone
with the mother
who had just given
birth to her. Nobody
said anything after
she finished
reading. The story
was terrifyingly
bad ("the-baby-
dies-in-'a-manger-
of-trash' bad,"
as one workshop
participant later
blogged) and none
of the students to skim
from the "midnight-
thick puddles" to where
"this brief mother's
child was born
breathless" could find
a failing in the tale
worth praise. Their
instructor was a poet
who had never cried
in a workshop, but
had felt like it before,
and had seen students
break down, one boy
tearing his poem
into strips as he wept,

his rants no more
original than what,
hand-written, he
shredded. The girl
who wrote the woman
into the alley with no
exit cried in the silence
of her fellow budding
writers. She cried for
herself as she left them
with the words, "I
quit"—left them
to their memories of
her failing that baby
she had composed to cry
out for all those the world
couldn't remember.

2.

But her failure
in their memories
was eclipsed the next
morning by an angel.
 "You will come to
know me as the angel
of death," this avenger
had promised in
the days before (as
the papers would
put it) "he stormed in,
opened fire, turned
the gun on himself."
This is the angel
who transfixed one
workshop writer
with his online self-
portraits, the barrelled
glare he unleashed on
her school. Held captive
before the screen
she relieved cigarettes
of every inch of ash
they withheld, asked
everyone who
messaged her why the credo,
"Live fast, die young,

104

and leave a mangled corpse,"
meant mangling leavings
and youth and speeds
beyond your own. This is
the angel at the sight
of which another
workshop writer
collapsed. Once he
had laughed at a child
on the news who, freed
from her captors,
seemed traumatized less
by the gunfire and
more by the fact
that Harry Potter
had not swept down
with a spell to save her.
He wished he had
thought more deeply about
the words we award
to terror, the phrases
embraced before body-
making boundaries
were effaced with so little
effort. After the attack,
he kept a list. There was
what his granny
had said about cancer's
advance. There was
the palm that a man
who could have been
testing the heat
and feel of the breeze
raised against
tanks. And in time
he would gather more
phrases, the "I love u
guys" Emily Keyes
texted to her family
from the desk in which
her murderer held her
hostage, and what
Jamie Rose Bolin
repeated years
later, though not
at fault, struck by her
killer for no other

reason than being
a child, "I'm sorry."

3.

In the days after
Kimveer Gill attacked
Dawson College,
slaying Anastasia De
Sousa. Himself. More
angels emerged for
the writing class. The
angel a friend sketched
for the victim on
a cyber-memorial
inspired a meditation
on "the childish shapes
cumulus takes along
eternity's most legible
seams." The shutterbug
shot her school tied shut
with police tape and altered
the pixeled images:
adding angels
to grip and raise the
ribbon as though
protecting those sickos
who find obscenity in
life laid nude. She
replaced "Police Line /
Do Not Cross" with
"Class of 2006," then
paved over "Class of"
with metres of yellow
brick road ("because,"
as the saying went,
"there is no place
like home"). The guy
who loved comics
drew a strip whose hero
had the power
to translate anything
into everything
else, the power to catch
Kimveer's bullets
in his teeth and

transform them
miraculously into a
voice, into sounded out
syllables, a sentence
that stirred words rather
than deafened them.

4.

"Every angel is
terrifying,"
the workshop instructor
quoted to begin
the poem she wrote for
the vigil. Classes would
exhume them the next
morning, reanimate the
day-to-day, and she
began the next
morning's work early,
reciting a lie: "Angels
are made terrifying by
what they protect us
from, like wicks
scorched to slake
darkness . . ." What
would sound evil to
the crowd is the modern
angelology of her
lectures. Forget God's
death—the angels are
alive and indifferent,
our cries to them as faint
as words in a burned
book are to the breeze
that un-pieces
the ashes. Under
the plenitude
of their hierarchies
the amassing matter
of our work and rage
composes a particle,
infinitesimal and
hidden, a smudge far
below the speeding
ceiling of the universe

in which nothing more
than a face or the outline
of some raw tool
is disclosed if
an angel spots it by
chance, stares long
enough, squinting just
so. Are we best embracing
this abandonment?
The danger the
instructor warned her
students against was
making angels of
ourselves, indifferent
and infallible, perfect
caretakers for the most
inhuman memorial,
the one that reads, "In
memory of in memory
of." There was a wisdom
the mind gained,
freeing thought to echo
or die in the gap
between itself and
the angels. There was
what she felt as she
returned from
the podium to
the crowd, the longing
for one of these things
to descend, to take her
up like a marionette
whose loamy joints
dragged their toes
endlessly from
Anastasia's vigil to
the un-vigiled waning
of all the too-soon
departed, from
Kimveer's unremarked-
upon burial to the shoe-
filled ditches and
shredded tents
that dapple the land-
scapes never painted
and framed to
commemorate

a community's birth.
There was grieving,
tending to the invisible
missing, and then
there's the chorus angels
could arrange. Imagine
a puppet conducting raids
on silence, plundering
the abyss with a song
for the names we wish
to keep briefly from
oblivion with our singing.

5.

The alley overflowed
with people. The people
packed the surrounding
streets. Those within
earshot of the woman
in labour whispered
encouragement. Those
drawn by the gathering
of a crowd heard
the rumour of
a birth. Waiting was all
any of them could
do. The girl who quit
the creative writing
class had revised
her story. On the bus
to school she counted
the copies, one
for each classmate
if the instructor would
have her. It was
the first class after
the attack. The alley
overflowed in defiance
of what she had written,
what she had known
as necessary, the crowd
ready to tend to whatever
burttling sliver of sun
might need to be passed
from hand to hand to hand.

Interlude

MORS FINIS NON EST (WHY WALLACE WROTE SUCH GOOD BOOKS)

What do you say if you just shouted "Victory for the Forces
of Democratic Freedom!" right when you came?
—David Foster Wallace

           That's the first sentence
you remember after hearing the news, of all the things he wrote
that stuck with you, your friend having just called from upstairs
with the headline when (of every question he'd asked
in his sadness and in his jest) you remember it. And you keep it
to yourself, your recollection of that question, as your friend reads
the article, gives you what a man on TV would call the few details
so far to "come out," to "emerge," as though they were felons
(the details) pinned in the woods before spotlights and pistols
and forced to surrender themselves and speak. What you wonder
is what he would do with it, this question coming to you
when it did, right before you understood, "got it," and the deluge
hit, you finally believing the fact you had met with total
disbelief. This paralysis that constricts in paralysis,
he'd see it first: your immobility before the whats and whys
and hows of this loss, and the more petty terror you feel, trapped
in the embarrassment of getting hung up on this one chance
line.
           In Wallace's poem
the felons would refuse to surrender, submitting
in their silence to oblivion instead. At most
they'd be lovers who puzzled their pursuers
with the sound they made when they made
love, the senseless victory
           they cried out for. Your friend
would call down in the end from upstairs. What
do you say?

We want the devil to be right. "Time and place can't change
the brain," is Satan's saying, the mind and self the brain contains
capable of making hell heaven and heaven hell. Wallace's genius
is this: his sentences prove the devil's vision of mind false
and true. This is more than a paradox or a game

or "masturbation." This is our burden. For though the mind possesses
the unclassifiable appendage of its own noisy void—the hand
and mouth and wing-like thing no community can clothe—
it still stretches flat for screening chatter-filled films, for light
cast so seductively through a celluloid-shouted "Enjoy!"
that not a single synapse dares to stray. This is why to speak
of a language is to speak of a way of death. It's why
in each ascent for the apical the ladders of our ideas leave us
stranded on the ledge of what we scaled, formulating plans
in the dirt and grieving scruffy and mad and singed beneath
these season-crushed skies. Many of us decide to climb our palms raw
against the mountain's sheer face, as though the rocks we cling to
are the features of our master's looking, suffocated by a surface
of stone. While those of us who quit the climb turn our eyes
closed instead or open on that final step that falls on nothing
but its fall. We want death to *not* be the end. And
it isn't. Death comes after. The end is first, within us from the start,
invisible and un-kindled except where it turns to spirals
all the straight lines we limn, the paths we draft in answer to
the "how do" and "how should" of the lives we fill with life.

                                   He ended like this. Not
another word. No more books. Behold

the man. Where he stood. Then
                           didn't. Where my friend read
his wife found him. I wonder what
he would have done. Which actions would he have decided to remain
undecided on? Hearing the news. This man who ogled endlessly
the infinity of the self, its escapes and cages, the closest he ever came
to saying "No" being a measured rejection of the spectacle's
relief, declining to be a part of it, even
                                   as a witness, what
would he have said, right now, "Look," or "Look
away"?

Research Material for Poetry on Late 20th-Century Art

April 15, 2007

My friend,

I hope this finds you well. Thank you for the letter. I have done what I can to answer your question, which I include here for your reference: "How should artists speak of events that refuse speaking—from Auschwitz to Rwanda, from colonization to colonization, from hurricane to tsunami?"

As an artist you need to feel your era in your bones, but, as you point out, how does one express this era when it is "appallingly," in Susan Sontag's words, "an age of genocide"? How does one bear witness in the way one is capable when confronted with what Theodor Adorno observed: that after Auschwitz there can be no more poetry? "Even the most extreme consciousness of doom," he wrote, "threatens to degenerate into idle chatter."

The dilemma—that to demand silence before these events is to remain quiet about the injustice that engenders them, while to speak, to render in words what was witnessed and remembered, is to risk tourism and appropriation. As you wrote me, "The future peoples who would build monuments to Silence, who would erect them lightyears away from any memory of the dead, are as frightening as the peoples who would reanimate mass graves for the sake of selling soap."

I believe the answer to your question resides in this imagining. Don't you find in your hypothesizing "future peoples" a potential voice, one that not only avoids but also investigates the silence and exploitation you fear? Why not begin by creating works that attend to the forms of language and life that bear witness to mass loss, that attempt to tally and transform the absences wrought by these disasters and crimes? However inchoate, they make what is gone material; they speak, though stuttering or scheming, what is otherwise unsaid.

Please find enclosed in this package the examples I composed for you, this "Research Material for Poetry on Late-Twentieth-Century Art." The peoples I have imagined are different artists: the art collective, the digital photographer, the filmmaker, and the cosmetic surgeon. In order to explore these artists, I have melded the poet's purview with a selection of respected cultural intermediaries: the scientist, the historian, the critic, and the eyewitness. The works I created for you are titled and ordered as follows:

1) Excerpt (1pg): American Institute for Retrieval. "Cup on the Table in Photo of Chernobyl." *In Nuce: A Complete Guide to Unknown Masterworks of World Culture*. Vol. 11. New York: CSH, 2002. 294-5.
2) Footnote (2pg): Cole, Stewart. "Rachel Whiteread and the Things of Emptiness." *In the Tower of No Shadows: Terror, the Sublime and 21st Century Art*. London: Verso, 2004. 127-28.
3) Review (3pg): Lim, Mi-Jin. "If This Is the Experiment, then the Results Are Not Good." Rev. of *Reg N. Rutrok's An Experiment in Living: Footage for a Documentary Film of the Tutsi Resettlement*, dir. Reg N. Rutrok. *The Times Herald* 20 Sep. 1997: R2.
4) Missive (2pg): Portner, Aaron. "Dear Anna, I hope." Greeting Card to Anna Hazel Collins. 23 Aug. 1999. The SAND Papers. The Canadian Museum for Human Rights Lib., Winnipeg.

To return to your question, how do we speak of the horror that demands, while refusing, voice? By imagining the hungers and ends of those who seek to define for us in relation to disaster what is real, what is just, what is possible and preserved. We speak by renewing poetry at the roots, seeking a new elegy to mourn the victims of a new breadth of murder, a new form of prophecy for glimpsing a new twilight's rise. Let the dogmatic and homogenized language that poetry opposes crack open poetry's own homogeneity and dogmatism and, hopefully, sound something new. Compose letters that answer questions with questions like "Will you give this a shot?" which is why I have written you and await your reply.

Sincerely yours,

Daniel Scott Tysdal

and, finally, to codify and assay the disaster's various remainders and resonances through all means available. Yet despite this propitious goal, the men's work was far from exhaustive.

Most prominently, the cup on the table in the photo of Chernobyl went unnoticed by the men who shared with the cup in the photo's endurance [3]. The men descending with instruments upon the apartment's dining room sought only what the dirt and air retained, a decade later, of disaster, the leavings that deceived all the senses but the ones they straight-out destroyed. The men in their protective, plastic second-skins gleaned nothing of the cup's origin and perseverance, of the life it had waited to sustain in those final shades of delay, the first signs of danger, when the cup's last bearer's finest textures were already changed in the mounting of what it knew too late as the failure to get away.

Within the 10,389 kg (4722 lb) of the men's data and analysis that we were able to examine, the appearance of the cup is limited to the photo with the men, and a brief description of the cup in a crate titled, "Things with Things Painted on Them," which reads as follows:

> 45E983H7: PORCELAIN TEACUP: (DIMENSIONS ILLEGIBLE): PASTORAL SCENE IN BLUE ON CUP'S OUTSIDE IS REPEATED LINE-FOR-LINE INSIDE THE CUP: THE SHORE OF A CIRCUMFERENCE-CIRCLING BROOK IS SPOTTED WITH BUSHES, COTTAGE, AND A LONE FISHERMAN KNEELING BY THE WATERS IN SEARCH OF FOOD.

The revocation of our archive privileges, coupled with the

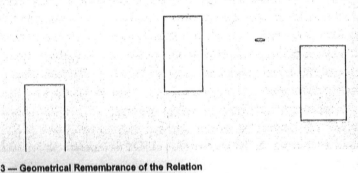

3 — Geometrical Remembrance of the Relation between the Cup and the Men in the Photo
Silver-gelatin print, 26 x 18.3 (10¼ x 7¼)

▲ 2110   ● 428 B.C.

4 — Gestural Sketch from Memory of the Cup in the Photo
Acrylic and photoemulsion on canvas, 149.9 x 114.3 (59 x 45)

5 — Ash between Glass
Ash and Glass, 1 x 1 (0.39 x 0.39)

levelling of the apartment complex (once the men had preserved and appraised everything they needed), left us only with the few capitalized and perspicuous lines we copied down from them, and our shared but separate memories of the way the cup in the photo held on **[4]**.

And lacking evidence, we remain divided on whether or not the cup can contain itself, whether there is more to the cup than the cup can hold. Among us are lives that want to decide the cup's convergence in duty with the cupping together of their own two hands. And though we've painted portraits of a Saviour lifting the cup to his lips, we cannot decide from which side he would sip in resigning Himself to the flavours the mortality of immortality literally offers up to itself. (One of us dreamed she fell with cups unblinking for eyes and the motion she descended on was the effortless motion light defines in its eternal composition of shadows.)

Some have speculated (without mentioning their wonder) that in the cup's painted scene, on the cottage's top floor, there is a window that when opened reveals a room with a table with a cup resting upon it. And on this cup the fisherman has carved all the names elided by the simple fact of being borne into days that pass. Name after name atop name he's scratched so all that remains is the porous poise of the cup's most raw and impractical twilight.

Others believe the figure kneeling by the brook is not fishing at all but simply sounding his few notes with the hum each ruin relays in the botched ascension of oblivion, in the singed strangeness of casting the endless disorder of his own ashes **[5]** over the waters that surge motionless before him, durable in blue,

▲ 1609, 1937

for them to carry with them into the morning" (386).[56]

---

[56] Stallabrass' anecdote, confirmed by a number of sources, is
not the only evidence to link Whiteread to Alana Grace. Grace
is the "acquaintance" Whiteread discusses in her 1999 BBC
interview with David Smith. In response to Smith's comment
about the tendency among young artists to construct their own
gallery spaces, Whiteread explains how

> a young acquaintance of mine once did that
> in a roundabout way. You see, she erased
> herself, with a computer, from all her family
> photos. Vacation shots, baby shots, school
> shots—she hung them in, like, her folks'
> kitchen, or their bedroom, it all had
> something to do with a friend of hers who'd
> gone and hopped off a bridge covered in
> class photos, or, no, that was a different
> moment. But this friend of mine never ended
> up offing herself, which I think had been
> part of the deal, because when her aunt, an
> artist, this aunt found all the emptied out
> pictures. She thought it was just brilliant.
> And advertised the kitchen or bedroom or
> whatever as a show. (3)

Further evidence of their relationship is the letter
Whiteread sent to "The Unpainter of Modern Strife," which is
on file in the Rossetti Archive at the Slade School of Art. In it
she thanks Grace for the edited stills of the Kennedy
assassination, the president's body, both pre- and post-
shooting, wiped clear from different views on the motorcade.
Whiteread adds that she is looking forward to receiving the
stills of Archduke Ferdinand removed from the carriage in
which he was shot and expired.

Not only has there never been any work done on
Whiteread's relationship with Grace, but little has been said
about Grace in the now developing cannon of 1990s visual
culture. Mortimer Prentice justifies Grace's exclusion in the
introduction to *Digit*, his anthology of computer generated art.

Grace, he observes, though an originator at the young age of 18, fell behind too quickly:

> By the time she was producing her assassination stills, Theresa Kolakowski had already completed her manipulations of the Zapruder film, while Matthew C. Holdenried was well into his epic salvaging of the Vietnam War with footage from WWII. (24)

Kolakowski's Zapruder, in which Jackie, Connelly, the car, et. al., are erased from the Dealey Plaza roadway (so that Kennedy alone floats past a crowd of waving then terrified witnesses), and Holdenried's new Vietnam, in which the 1940's Yankee G.I. replaces his Dawning of the Age of Aquarius counterpart in combat footage, render Grace's work, for Prentice, "short-sighted and amateurish, and, in a way, obsolete" (24).

Grace, in the final blog entry she left before removing herself from public view, contrasts Prentice's view with her own peculiar theory:

> All these tragedies. I will now and forever take the blame for them. You all holed [sic] me responsible for 9/11 and I won't argue. You say I prayed for towers to erase and bless you with planes that combust spontaneously mid-flight in a sky. Can you imagine if it had been raining that day?

Grace recently took a government job editing internet photos of sexually abused children whose whereabouts are unknown. She erases the child, what is done to the child, so that purified and unpeopled surroundings can be released to the public to give those who might have visited those rooms (with no idea (without them) what happened there) the chance to tell the proper authorities where to look.

128

If This Is the Experiment, then th

MI-JIN LIM
ON THE LINE

On May 12, 1943, Polish Jew Szmul Zygielbojm took his own life as World War II raged on and news of the horrors of the camps reached the Allied communities. What is important to remember about Zygielbojm's act, as he states in his letter to the former leaders of his occupied home, is that he committed suicide not in response to the cruelty of the camps but as a reaction against the world's response to this cruelty. Horror was met only by silence; violence by indifference. Even the Polish government, who Zygielbojm admits did more than anyone to raise public awareness about the camps, "did not do anything that was not routine, that might have been appropriate to the dimensions of the tragedy taking place." The horror and evil would have been bearable had an at least equivalent force of good arisen in reply, a benevolent undertaking as shocking and unconventional as the unconventional and shocking malevolence of the camps. That Zygielbojm believed his death might constitute such a reply, and "contribute to destroying the indifference of those who were able to act [but chose not to]," evidences both the depth of his faith in humanity and his naiveté

A figure in the jungle awaits its fate in *Reg N. Rutrok's An Experiment in Film of the Tutsi Resettlement*

about the vigour of the self-interest that seems to guide our kind.

My review, though not a suicide note, does share in Zygielbojm's dilemma. Where he was shocked by the global apathy that met the news of the camps, I am shocked by the accolades and praise that have been showered upon an evil (which, I know, I write at the risk of sounding fanatical) film. Where for Zygielbojm the camps exampled "how little human life was worth" in his age, *Reg N. Rutrok's An Experiment in Living: Footage for a Documentary Film of the Tutsi Resettlement* expresses, for me, pretty much the same thing. Unequivocally, no film (no cultural

artefact, past or present, for that matter) has brought me closer to doubting the capacity of our species to not only empathize and commune but to survive. That a number of my peers have had the audacity to describe this film as "irreverent but honest," "bold," "unflinching," and "a must-see," is shameful and, frankly, beyond comprehension.

For those of you who don't know the origins of Rutrok's project, *An Experiment in Living* performs the contemptible act of contemporizing the unreleased Nazi propaganda film *Theresienstadt: A Documentary Film of the Jewish Resettlement*. *Theresienstadt*, marking an abuse of cinematic technology

ent, then the Results Are Not Good

Reg N. Rutrok's An Experiment in Living: Footage for a Documentary

artefact, past or present, for that matter) has brought me closer to doubting the capacity of our species to not only empathize and commune but to survive. That a number of my peers have had the audacity to describe this film as "irreverent but honest," "bold," "unflinching," and "a must-see," is shameful and, frankly, beyond comprehension.

For those of you who don't know the origins of Rutrok's project, *An Experiment in Living* performs the contemptible act of contemporizing the unreleased Nazi propaganda film *Theresienstadt: A Documentary Film of the Jewish Resettlement. Theresienstadt*, marking an abuse of cinematic technology

until now unmatched, was filmed at the concentration camp of the same name by German-Jewish actor, writer and director Kurt Gerron (from whose name, anagramically, the pseudonym Reg N. Rutrok is derived). A friend of such luminaries as Marlene Dietrich and Peter Lorre, Gerron ended up in Theresienstadt after underestimating the Nazi threat and refusing to escape to America. During the making of his film, Gerron staged well-attended public events at the camp, such as debates, concerts and soccer games; he coaxed malnourished and terrified children into playing happily; he asked fellow prisoners to carry out before the camera the simple routines

of a daily life that had been stolen from them. The challenge put to him by the Nazis was to show the world that a concentration camp, specifically, a camp that lay on the road to Auschwitz, was, in "truth," a kind of Jewish city-state, a little utopia that greatly improved upon the traditional ghettos.

An Experiment in Living shares with *Theresienstadt* the same twisted goal, to misrepresent a genocide (in this case, Rwanda, 1996) as an act of compassionate social engineering; yet where Gerron aimed for propagandic purity, in the sense that he sought to conceal the painful facts of his material under an ideal and generic façade, Rutrok seeks to document material that no technological trick or generic conceit could ever transfigure or contain. As unbelievable as this may sound, *An Experiment in Living* is *Theresienstadt* as remade in the showers and ovens of Auschwitz. Rutrok attempts to reshape the massacre of the Tutsi in the Rwandan jungles into a utopic cause the same way Gerron tried to reshape the Nazi's project of liquidation into a philanthropic gesture. Rutrok literally directs the violence; he makes "players" out of the victims and a stage out of the slaughter. And since this is "footage" for a documentary film, and not the edited, narrated, subtitled, and scored final cut, we "get to hear" Rutrok direct a father, who is about to be butchered, as he begs for his son's life; we are "given" the different angles Rutrok takes on the Tutsi woman tied up and unconscious behind the home of her Hutu captor.

As I've already suggested (and, as consumers of various news media, I'm sure you are already aware), the shock expressed by my peers is negligible. After going through the motions of the required "compassionate" caveats, they promote *An Experiment in Living* promote *An Experiment in Living* as a "chilling meditation on the cinema's relationship to terror," as "the ultimate deconstruction of the documentarian's claim to object-iveity," "a sobering indictment of our times," and on and on and on and on. Sadly, along with guesses over Rutrok's true identity (he still has not come forward despite receiving special mention at the recent New York Film Festival), the only struggle that unites my peers is the one over "essential" questions regarding the film's authenticity. Many of them have gathered evidence from the film's five and a half hours in order to prove why or why not he or she believes the events filmed are genuine or staged, without once wondering: does it matter? I mean, is there really a difference between the two possibilities, "real" or "fake," in the face of the more important question: should this film have even been made?

And before answering too quickly (again, "fanatic" warning) please consider that what is at stake in your response is not simply the potential for a kind of cultural experience but the survival of the very qualities that make us cultured beings. So rather than give you another apathetic review, I ask that you give me the chance to compose a reply (borrowing Zygielbojm's phrasing) that is "appropriate to the dimensions of the tragedy taking place." I want the chance to tell you why I believe that what *An Experiment in Living* offers us is evidence that our passion for the freedom of individual expression and con-sumption (in which the popular practices of transgression and subversion, of nihilism and irreverence (and your "fanatical" reviewer will go as far as to include our prohibition against censorship), are based) threatens to "transgress" and "subvert" all limits and boundaries until this passion for the self has erased forever the very individual that is capable of experiencing and exercising the freedom to create and consume. (*Continued on R5*)

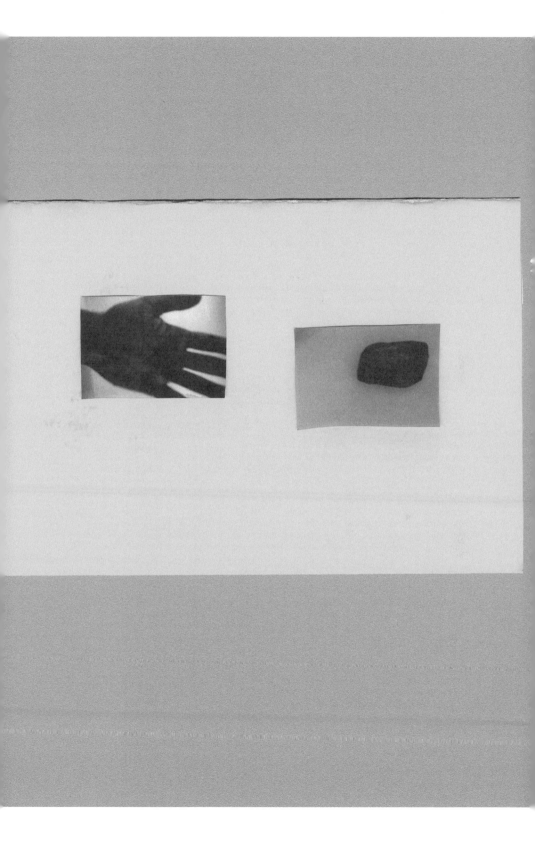

23/08/99

Dear Anna,

I hope this finds you well. I spoke to your mom earlier today and she gave me your address. It's great to hear you're doing your residency in California. Congratulations.

I'm also living on a west coast these days, in Freetown, the capital of Sierra Leone. All in all, it's a lot like any coastal city. From the room I rent I can see rooftops, and beyond them the ocean, the sun just starting to set. A few minutes before I sat down to write you a children's street band passed below my window, slapping sticks together and beating their improvised drums. I've been here for about two months now, volunteering with the "Scars Are the New Diamonds" Project. I came at the invitation of Jean-Marc, who's almost put in a full year of service with the Project. Since I never ended up returning to school I'm not involved with him in the O.R., but working in the field is fine with me.

Your mom couldn't say enough about the work being performed here, which, I know, she did for my benefit, but it's good to hear people back home are being reached. She says instead of a ring, she's thinking of asking your father for one of those bullet wound scars for their anniversary. Like the rest of the volunteers, I had one grafted to my pinkie upon arriving and told her it only hurt a bit before healing.

As you can imagine, my work is exhausting. But I don't hate it. Today I signed up a donor who agreed to give the footlong scar from his thigh in exchange for the usual benefits. A lawyer in Massachusetts has already paid over a hundred grand to have the scar grafted across his chest, something like a sash. The donor told me that his leg was cut off below the knee by the rebels when he refused to take part in the fighting.

One of the perks of the job is that even though a majority of the Project's procedures take place in the states, most of the celebrities get their work performed here in Freetown. Jean-Marc let me sit in while he grafted the scar from a toddler's forehead to the cheek of the guitarist from that band you used to love. Some rebels had bet on the toddler's sex before cutting her out of her mother's stomach so, really, it's a miracle she lived. It was her brother who gathered her out of the jungle, her tiny head bleeding, and the guitarist promised to show off the scar and tell the tale of her plight every chance he got.

nThough I want to say that you shouldn't feel obliged to write back, I would really like it if you did, earth-shattering news or otherwise. I wouldn't actually mind hearing something simple. For example: do you ever walk to the beach to watch the way the sun dissolves in distant waters? Do you still listen to that guitarist and his band before falling asleep each night? XXX
XXXXXXXXXXXXXXXXXXXXXXXXXXXXXXXXXXXXXXXXXXXXXXXX

I made the card myself. I hope you like it. The pictures on the front are the palm I tried grafting a passion fruit flower's broken stamen to. And the scar from my shoulder (remember that fall?), I pinned it repeatedly to this same, small stone, but it refused to hold.

Yours always,

Aaron

The Open Toll

THEREMINIST SING THE BODY PLASTIC

for Albert "Slim" Redstone's visit to Body Worlds in Taipei, Taiwan

Oh my Body!
        —Walt Whitman

1. The exhibit is alien enough for a thereminist. And Slim
would welcome that otherworldly trill, one of those
ghost-voiced scores from films with titles like *The Day
the Earth Stood Still*, *Mars Attacks!* That would make sense.
Aliens doing this: turning a tarred lung plastic, making
a skinned man's hide plastic for him to offer in his plastic
muscled grasp, making plastic

                              the dead. Slim waits for them
to show, these aliens, emerging tentacled or bipedal
with moon-shaped skulls to fuse plastic with his skin, flayed, say,
after they torture him. "Admit we've saved you," they'd demand
before preserving each of his wounds, his flesh peeled back
into thousands of tiny mouths sticking their tiny tongues out

at decay. He reaches for the cheek of a plastinated boy
when no one but the boy is looking, and he wonders if
the aliens are right there, genuinely synthetic beneath
his touch, feeding on the boy's decomposing decomposition,
an alien, like a parasite, perceptible only where it mangles its home.

2.   Slim had made a monster of himself
by mistake. That was on the evening before he visited
Body Worlds. He had meant to clean up, shaving the stubble
from his face and scalp. But the hot water at the hotel
hadn't worked. The razor scraped his skin and the cold water,
polluted, harboured microscopic creatures that infiltrated
his pores and festered, crowning him with a laurel of sores,
his jaw throbbing with crimson growth. His razor

couldn't clear it. In the gallery
                        he keeps his hood

up—a portal for curious patrons to peer in
as they withdraw from
display after display.
                              Only one completes the quest,
pressuring Slim's infection with enough touch to ask, "Real?"

3.   Slim answers, "Yes
and no." He submits to the exhibit its lone animate form.
His dream? To be printed on gift shop puzzles with
the plastic muscled man who clutches his plastic skin
like an overcoat, holds it out as if to say, "There will
never be another rain." Along with the anonymous departed
parted into pieces, Slim longs to be taken apart by
children for $7.99 and pieced together again. He doesn't need

a name or an age or a time and space of death and birth.
As the museum's director said, "Those details
are distracting. They tend to just make people feel
sorry." Slim searches for PA systems, the plastinated
thunder of some storm, anything to amplify his cry:
"See this beast's plastinated mouth cut off from
our language!" "See this beast's plastinated heart
cut off from what we love!" But Slim knows

                                        this is false
advertising, a close-up on a scab that blinds you to miles
of uniting veins. The gallery-goers
are cut off together from their ghastly crew, the useless tools
                              of their razed limbs.
                              There should be this
                              smell. The smell
                                        the dead

make. The gallery is an SS dream—a clinical mass no mask
or bulldozer is needed to bury. "Without this stink the dead
can't move us," Slim whispers to the suffering bored, the tourists
in their amusement
                    exclaiming "Dŭ?!" (which translates
as "See"). The dead should enter what we breathe
as what we breathe enters us. Would he be wrong
to vomit in the billowing of a total lack of stench?

4.

What is a body

world? The brain is a skin beneath the skin of a baby. A baby
a skin beneath the skin of its mom. If the body is a world
then it's born where things and the brain in the baby in the mom
commune, resound, collide . . . what's the word? There

isn't just one. The sulcus and gyrus of world are the baby
of brains and things—the skin
of their entanglement. Once

the story of Mother and Child led us to believe the horizon
of total love, the total force of Creation could be contained
in a womb's mortal span—one woman, right there, held
everything.
              Before Slim, the mother now reclines. She's posed
doubly nude in her muscle, one skinned arm like an actor's bent
to affect disinterest in being the newest beauty, the other hand
frozen mid-fidget without fingerprints, caught in a gesture
that begs, "Are we almost
done?" No.

No. She is posed triply
nude. Her stomach sliced
open on the boulder
of her baby. The baby
they crashed back into
this cratered birthplace.
                            If this is a crime against the body
                                       it is because time
is wronged. This is the body for a world
whose attention is fixed on the immortal now.
Past and future are rescinded worth
in this packaging where the dead
endure without substance, no womb
awaiting the future's unborn. "All the earth's frames
shall stand empty," the anonymous wanderer laments
centuries ago. The frames? Empty? The frames
are brawny, friend, and filled beyond your grief.

                                       Slim

123

5. you can't escape on the bus
you catch after the exhibit.
There's no such race
as the "away." Once a drop
of dew on civilization's bark
always a particle of breath
behind its growl. If only you could see how
the thereminist makes her instrument sing: the "L"
of the antennas burst with invisible waves her hands surf

conducting sound.

What you fear is the myth. The Legend of the Plastinators.
In their final phase they invent
a compound for transforming into marble
                                        the air. Which one
of your fellow commuters carries the recipe in his dreams? Or
the first sample in his pocket—it slips free, an accident,
and instantly you are commemorated, folded into the stony flesh
of the monument. Or you're half a world away when the air-fed
creation is delivered, leaving an hour before the mounting sheets
of marble crest: which pose
would you hold? Here's one:
                        It isn't her song that fits
the exhibit no matter how clearly it sings the moans
of a corpse newly risen shackled in plastic, sings
the sound of a resurrected heart labouring to pump
away polymers. Her posture stirs against the monstrosity

of the marble's tide. The aliens who ascend and chip you free
will know from your pose that even as every absence was effaced
one pair of hands sought pitches in the invisible, in the invisible
there were volumes we withdrew.

Outro

POETRY HERO

I'm so happy 'cause today I found my friends.
They're in my head.
                                    —Kurt Cobain

The fan felt the chorus of past mysteries howl
when she learned Cobain had taken his life:
the mystery of why her dad had done the same thing,
the mystery of how the fruit flies felt
a decade past when the science fair ended
and Mr. Anholt made her drown them in the sink.
Executives argued over what to launch first:
the unfinished sessions or the greatest hits.
Many fans lit candles. Others ashed
themselves in the music's ground zero,
the full-voiced vacuum of Nirvana-less dark.

Listen to Kurt's music explode in the coals
of cover bands and jamming high school kids,
the embers of karaoke-kindled joy,
the cinderish sediment of hands
tapping plastic buttons at the right time
to scorch Guitar Hero's highest score.
Lurking the country churchyard of fan sites,
herd the lowing glow of pixeled portraits,
the epitaphal drone of misquoted lyrics
counterpointed by necrophiliac fan fic.
A river ripped away your idol's final
resting place, the static of his ashes
dispersing through channels that widen
and disband in the sea, but it's still on this bank
that you must lay the memorial album
you cut, the cover your photoshopped shot
of a dollar bill in swimming-pool blue
trailing a baby impaled on a fish hook.

Ants tend to their dead. That's a well known fact.
The fallen are mountained in heaps above ground.
Less well known is the trick scientists play
on ant brains. Shot with a lab-fashioned scent,
living ants are taken for dead. Their conned
workmates carry them kicking to the colony's tomb.
The exiled try to return to their duties
under the earth but are banished as dead
again, buried in the untunnelable bulk
of sunshine and open air. The real art of greats
like Cobain is to play the opposite trick
on those of us who scavenge for scraps of their sight,
who drag back to the colony the shreds
of the carcass of a voice screaming full blast.

Poetry Hero is coming soon. In the age
of at-home lipo and the nano-meth fix,
the artist of our time will finally be extinct.
The need to create will not reach obsolescence
with new platforms and new programmable codes.
It's the object that we'll lose. The intimacy
of Poetry Hero's neuro-interface
will let you feel the exact peace and pain
Cobain felt composing his masterworks
before he made the rifle a mic that fired back.
You'll have the power to immerse yourself
in Milton, to feel the ruling joy, the servile
ambition he felt picking this word for that stress
to make *Paradise Lost* more beautifully lead
the world to choose freely their love for God.
All of us will be Shakespeare. All Gaga and Pound.
Even this very line can be yours
to compose just before the simulation ends
and the thing thrills you with your brilliance,
the screen not falling black until it is bright
with the lasting, flashing words, "You Win."

NOTES

The epigraphs, in order of appearance, are quoted from *Letters of Sigmund Freud*, Stephen Ziplow's *The Film Maker's Guide to Pornography*, G.W.F. Hegel's *The Phenomenology of Spirit*, *CNN.com*, Rainer Maria Rilke's *Duino Elegies*, David Foster Wallace's *Brief Interviews with Hideous Men*, Walt Whitman's "I Sing the Body Electric," and Kurt Cobain's "Lithium."

Earlier versions of some of these poems appeared in the magazines *dandelion*, *Descant*, *Eye Weekly*, *Matrix*, *Prairie Fire*, *PRISM international*, and in the anthologies, *Boredom Fighters*, *Fast Forward*, *GULCH*, and *Rogue Stimulus*.

ACKNOWLEDGEMENTS

Thanks and love to all of you who helped me with these poems, to Tightrope Books (particularly, Shirarose Wilensky and Karen "Prentice" Correia Da Silva), to Stewart Cole for his friendship and generosity, to my family (for everything), and to Andrea Charise (for everything, again).